TROUE
AT THE
WATERWORKS

'A Prostate Cancer Journey'

James Napier

Published by James Napier

©2015 James Napier

All rights reserved

ISBN 978 0 9571037 1 9

Designed by April Sky Design www.aprilsky.co.uk

Printed by GPS Colour Graphics Limited, Belfast

After 35 years in education, James Napier is now a full time author.

He has written a number of textbooks to support the work of science teachers and students in Northern Ireland, and a number of popular science books for the wider public.

In addition, he has written *Living on the Ledge*, a book raising awareness of attention deficit disorder (ADHD).

He is currently undergoing treatment for prostate cancer.

The author would like to thank all those who gave generously of their time to read earlier drafts and provided very useful feedback, in particular Catherine and Alan.

This book is dedicated to family members and friends who have been touched by cancer, and to the staff of the Cancer Centre in Belfast, particularly the radiotherapists who worked in LA9 through May – June 2014.

All proceeds from the sale of this book will be used to support the work of the *Friends of the Cancer Centre.*

Foreword

Prostate cancer is the most commonly diagnosed cancer in men. Approximately one in ten men in the UK will be diagnosed with this condition in their lifetime. Thankfully the treatment for prostate cancer has improved greatly in the past 10 years. In particular our ability to accurately target prostate cancer using modern radiotherapy machines (Linear Accelerators) along with powerful computer planning techniques such as Intensity Modulated Radiotherapy (IMRT) has meant better cure rates along with fewer side effects.

No two cancer journeys are the same. Everyone will have a slightly different reaction to the news that they have cancer. In this novel James describes how the obvious worry of the cancer diagnosis is counterbalanced by the fact there was treatment available. He also describes the patient's perspective on radiotherapy treatment and planning with a clear attention to detail.

As well as having the latest technology and expertise, a Cancer Centre can only really claim to be a centre of excellence if it also has an ethos of excellence running throughout the department. I am very proud of our Cancer Centre in Belfast and in particular the positive and friendly ethos of the radiotherapy staff. I think this ethos comes through in James' novel.

Professor Joe O'Sullivan
Clinical Director of Oncology
Belfast Health and Social Care Trust.

Chapter 1

On that particular Thursday there was more post than normal. There were two *Amazon* packets – slim books or CDs based on their shapes. The usual array of junk; supermarket savers and balance transfer offers from at least one credit card company. But it was the buff-coloured envelope that caught the eye. Probably yet another hospital appointment. The transparent address window and the characteristic 'hospital' font virtually confirmed its origin. Once the junk was binned or added to the shredding pile the *Amazon* packets were next on the list. Both were addressed to Jane, a nice surprise for her when she gets up.

Now for the hospital letter. Hopefully, it would be for a suitable day, avoiding the hassle of having to change the date. Scanning beyond the Health and Social Care and Hospital numbers, I quickly registered that the appointment was for the Urology Clinic on Thursday 5th December at 10 am. Couldn't be much better; Thursdays suited well and the timing meant that I would miss the worst of the traffic. The letter contained the usual admin details: *'Please ring to confirm that your appointment is suitable. As this is a teaching hospital, undergraduate students may be in attendance during your appointment, blah, blah'* and the usual warning about the implications of failing to attend without cancelling or amending the appointment.

There was just the one paragraph that was different – strange almost. It was the third one down, almost hidden by, and squeezed in between, the capitalised date, location and Consultant's name above, and the bold warning regarding missing appointments below.

It read: '*This appointment will give you an opportunity to discuss details with the Consultant. A friend or relative is welcome to accompany you*'.

First time I'd seen something like this in one of these letters. It is often hit or miss whether you see a Consultant or a Registrar at these appointments, so why emphasise the Consultant? And why would I need to bring a friend or a relative? Still, this can all be sorted out later. I added the details to my diary and made a mental note to confirm the appointment in the afternoon. Emptying the dishwasher and sorting breakfast were the immediate priorities. Everything else could wait.

Life was good at the moment. There was plenty of freelance work to keep me busy and 'semi-retirement' was much more relaxed than the grind and demands of full time work. Jane was still doing some translating and archive work but not enough to stop us getting away on short city breaks. At long last we now knew what the term 'chilling' meant.

I did confirm the appointment that afternoon, then tossed the letter into my bedside drawer. Hopefully, it wouldn't get lost in the ever increasing pile. There was so much bumph in it the drawer would hardly shut. The appointment was three weeks away, something to be forgotten about until closer to the time.

For November the weather was dire. Rain, storms and bitterly low temperatures seemed to be the order of the day. Global warming or what? The forecast gave snow for later in the week. You couldn't even get out for a good walk, let alone get out for a run in this. Not exactly brilliant for the mood.

At least sleeping was a bit easier in the colder nights. Or it was most nights. I still had to get up to nip to the loo at least twice, the usual older man thing. And of course at least one of the visits was in the dead of night, getting back to sleep then was in the lap of the gods. Why are we programmed to think, and worry, about things then that don't bother us during the day? It was on one of these occasions that I started to think again about the hospital letter. I was no stranger to these of course, particularly in recent years. But just how significant were those extra few ambiguous lines? Was it as innocent as it seemed? And why would I need to bring a friend or relative when I never have had to before? But this wasn't all - there were other differences. The letter arrived only two and a half weeks after the prostate biopsy. That is pretty quick by NHS standards. When I had my previous prostate biopsy (this one was my second) it took ages to get feedback. And on that occasion the letter from the hospital was very straightforward.

Surprisingly, I was able to dig out a copy of the follow-up letter from my first biopsy from a year or so ago. Not sure whether by design or accident – the filing cabinet was as chaotic as ever. It was much more to the point and it seems that my copy was just a courtesy copy of the letter sent to my GP. The key information was in one short paragraph.

'This gentleman has had a TRUS biopsy of the prostate. The biopsy did not show evidence of malignancy. There was a small amount of prostatic intraepithelial neoplasia. His IPSS score is 30 and he is currently on Combodart.

I have arranged flow rate investigations and a bladder scan.'

All very straightforward. A quick internet research reminded me that IPSS is an abbreviation for 'International Prostate Symptom Score' and that this is an indication of how much an individual is affected by prostate problems. It is based on a questionnaire involving features such as flow rate, urgency, and how quality of life is affected. While it is obviously subjective, it does give the medics a good idea of the degree of the problem, or to be more accurate, the degree of the problem as perceived by the patient. 30 was fairly high as far as I could remember.

The reference to prostatic intraepithelial neoplasia indicated that there were some abnormal cells, probably not malignant, but possibly abnormal enough to suggest a pre-cancerous state; cells that were not a problem at the moment, but cells that would need close watching in the future.

The difference between the two letters meant it was hard not to jump to conclusions. It was also going to be difficult to wait the three weeks until the appointment came around. Perhaps not, maybe I already knew the outcome.

Nonetheless, I would say nothing to Jane. No point in having her worried. Probably another man thing.

Chapter 2

Gail still missed her dad. She missed him a lot. He was an inspiration and a font of wisdom. Her mum was still alive. She loved her very much but it was not the same, for some reason she had seemed closer to him. He had been dead for seven years but it still seemed like yesterday – perhaps this is the way it is going to be. Particularly when special dates come around such as the anniversary of his death, which was the following day.

Still it was not all bad news. She and Steve were getting on well. They had just moved into a flat in the university area. Not bad after only getting together four months ago. Dad would have approved, he would like Steve. In fact Steve was very like him. I suppose this is what daughters do. They end up with someone like their dad.

Gail was on the early shift today and she and Steve were planning to go out to the pub later. That would lift her spirits. Only a couple of hours to go to home time.

Seeing her reflection in the glass of the revolving door as she left work for home, Gail acknowledged to herself that her hair needed some attention; it needed cutting, coloured, probably the lot. More expense. She was fairly slim but not being tall made her appear not quite as slim as she would have liked. Not when she compared herself to some of her trendy colleagues. Still, she concluded that she looked as well as most 24 year olds. Another bonus was that while she was both competent and enthusiastic in the workplace, she could leave it behind her as she walked through those revolving doors. Just as well, as she sees some sad cases in a typical day.

Although only November, Christmas was on the horizon. Not that presents had been bought, or any thought given to

Christmas arrangements, but it did add to the atmosphere in town. There were more people out at night and a greater buzz. Gail liked buzz, not surprising for someone who carried the feisty gene.

They had a quick bite to eat in the flat and headed for 'The Limit', a popular student pub that they still enjoyed. A great place to meet old mates. And 24 was not too old to be mixing with students. Steve ordered the cocktails (they often started with a cocktail each) as Gail found a spare table in the corner. They were lucky, in half an hour there would be very few seats left, never mind a table. And certainly, trying to order a cocktail when the place was busy was a nightmare.

Once organised, Steve suggested they have a toast to Gail's dad – he knew the significance of the date. Steve wasn't sure whether Gail would want to talk about him tonight but he needn't have worried. Toast over, Gail began reminiscing and started talking about her work.

'I love my job Steve, and my choice of career was influenced to a large extent by my dad. It wasn't obvious at the time but seeing him ill and in pain made me want to help people. And radiotherapy seemed the obvious choice. Just a pity that the pay is crap.'

Steve knew that Gail was well suited to work in a 'caring profession' and this helped explain the choice of radiotherapy, although he felt that he had known this anyway, or perhaps just assumed it. He thought she was bright enough to have been a doctor – at least they get well paid for their 'caring' – but this would have been a fruitless debate.

'Your dad died of bone cancer; is that not fairly rare?'

'He did have cancer of the bone but that stemmed from prostate cancer initially. The prostate cancer had spread into his bones. Like so many men he had plenty of warning signs;

running to the loo too often, a bit leaky on it, but he just didn't know they were warning signs. By the time he went to the doctor it was far too late. From then it was just a matter of time, and pain.'

Gail noticed an old friend at the bar, trying in vain to attract the barman's attention. She gave her a quick wave hoping she would come over for a chat when she had been served. Steve welcomed the potential diversion. He wanted the feisty Gail back. He knew that there was nothing like friendly company or going for a run to restore Gail's bubbly mood.

A couple of hours later they wandered home. Content. It had stopped raining and they were disciplined enough not to stop at any of the many fast-food joints on the way. Tomorrow and the workplace were really not that far away. Although neither of them thought they would be getting to sleep anytime soon.

Chapter 3

It was hard to sleep on the night of 4th December. The wind was howling, bins were crashing over, gates banging and windows rattling. Anticipating the mess to be sorted in the morning didn't encourage sleep. Nor did tomorrow's hospital appointment.

Over the last week I had dropped a few hints to Jane about my thoughts on how the day would go. She was pragmatic, 'what will be will be, and no point reading too much into the letter. Still it would be good to get it out of the way, remove the uncertainty.' Agreed on that one.

Just for a change I decided to go to Belfast by train, rather than take the car. It was a short walk to my local station and the hospital had its own stop. The wind had dropped and it was chilly but bright, ideal winter walking conditions. Easier to think on the train.

The Department of Urology was on Level 3 in the hospital. A short walk from the train halt, through the main hospital entrance, turn left and take the lift to the Third Floor. I was there in good time, handed my appointment letter to the receptionist and took a seat in the small waiting area. There were some nice paintings on the wall – local landscapes – which added to the homely feel. Being an early appointment, it was likely that things would run fairly close to time. A bit like the dentists, you are more likely to be taken on time for a 9.30 appointment than for a 4.30 one. On cue, I was called right on time.

I was shown into a small consulting room with bright yellow walls. The Consultant was sitting at his computer at the far side of the room. He had a friendly face and demeanour. I was followed in by what I assumed to be a nurse. As soon as I was seated she closed the door and took a seat herself. Two of them to fill me in, another novelty. Pleasantries were exchanged with the Consultant. A bit surreal. Then it was time for action.

'Jack, the results came back positive.'

I knew what he meant, but mischievously thought about replying, 'brilliant, glad the news is great – I'm glad it's positive news.' I wonder how he would have reacted to that. But of course, I knew what he meant. I just had to wait for him to confirm it. Then came the positives.

'We think your prostate cancer will be treatable. We are sure we have caught it in time. In due course we will need to discuss treatment options, but that is not for today. Today is really about helping you come to terms with the fact that you have cancer. It will probably take you a while to fully digest this news.'

Too right, I thought. At this point, Mr Jackson – I always found it strange that Consultants reverted back to Mr or Mrs – introduced his colleague, who was sitting quietly just inside the door. She was a specialist oncology nurse and she would be my 'named' specialist nurse through all aspects of the treatment. Good to hear, but I suspect one of her roles is to mop up those patients who struggle to cope with bad news and sweep them off for a coffee, or well out of sight anyway, once the Consultant has done his bit. A nice blend of humanity or efficiency, depending whether coming from patient or NHS perspective.

Mr Jackson then said he would take me through the pathologist's report. He had already called it up on the screen, almost certainly to refresh his memory of the facts before I came in. In effect, he told me that five out of twelve of the tissue samples taken were cancerous. All the cores from the left side of the prostate were positive as was one from the right hand side. The approximate size of the tumour was 10 mm. I assumed that it was all the one tumour, rather than two or more? There was evidence of perineural invasion he said – this meant that the cancer cells were tracking along the nerve that leads out of (or into) the prostate. He explained that the perineural invasion may be significant. The nerve enters the prostate through a small gap in the surrounding prostate capsule; the capsule being a protective cover, but also often an important barrier to cancer spread. It wasn't hard to work out that if the cancer cells were tracking along the nerve surface they could just as easily track their way out of the small gap along with the nerve. If the cancer had spread beyond the prostate we were in a different scenario. But we weren't going to find out one way or another today. There was just enough said to leave doubt.

Mr Jackson explained that the next step was to go home and think about treatment options, most likely radiotherapy or surgery. Both have significant side effects and these needed to be talked through with Jane. Meanwhile, he will organise scans to confirm the extent of the tumour and to try to identify if the cancer has in fact spread beyond the prostate, additional factors that will have an impact on treatment options. At this stage the specialist nurse gave me a load of support leaflets in a nice little purple folder. I had a quick look at the first two; 'Prostate cancer – A guide for newly diagnosed men' and 'Living with and after prostate cancer – A guide to physical, emotional and practical issues' – I liked the reference to 'after'! Both leaflets were provided by Prostate Cancer UK. Plenty of time to read all this. And that was that. After a few pleasantries I was on my way. In the waiting room there were two men, both with partners, and both looked just a bit older than myself. What was their news going to be? Did the Consultants bring all the 'positives' in together and get all this week's bad news over at the one time? I was tempted to wait and see if they were followed into the room by the oncology nurse, but that would be pointless, so I checked my train times and headed back to the halt.

I was in a bit of a daze as I walked down to catch the train. Would life now be defined as life before and life after diagnosis? And we didn't really know if the cancer had spread as yet or what sort of prognosis there was. I wasn't really sure how I felt. When I finally collapsed into a window seat on the train I began to replay the events that had led up to today. I wasn't even sure where to start.

Chapter 4

I cannot really remember when I wasn't running to the loo during the night. This probably means I cannot really remember when I didn't have prostate issues. It had been there in the background, a long-running hassle that was not quite annoying enough to force me to do anything about it. I think medical input began about five or six years ago. I was attending the GP for something else – probably stomach problems – and raised the issue, almost in passing.

'I am running to the loo at night – at least twice' (the 'at least twice' for emphasis).

'Are you getting up more often, or has it always been like this?'

'Not really sure, but I think I might be getting up more.'

Not exactly scientific, but I think this got the ball rolling. The GP's response was fairly predictable and no doubt one he has made many times.

'We'll take some blood and get a PSA test done. The results should be back in less than a week. If there is anything out of the ordinary I'll give you a ring, otherwise I'll be seeing you in a month's time anyway to see how you are getting on with those new stomach tablets. Right Jack, let's get that sleeve rolled up.'

I didn't ask Dr Woods what a PSA test was – I didn't want to appear stupid. Should be easy to check this up on the Internet. What else is the internet for? Perhaps the cancer charity websites would be the best place to start.

PSA is an abbreviation for prostate-specific antigen. The test measures the amount of PSA, a small protein made by the prostate, in the blood. It is naturally present in the blood in very, very small quantities – it is measured in nanograms per millilitre of blood (ng/ml). A nanogram is very small – 10^{-9}

grams, nearly too small for most people to comprehend. A 'normal' value for someone under sixty is a reading of 3 ng/ml or less, although the amount in the blood tends to increase as people get older. Although there are a number of factors that can cause raised PSA values, significantly higher values are often associated with prostate cancer.

It was reassuring to have got as far as having the test done. Even more so for Jane, who had been suggesting this for some time, almost agitating for me to have a PSA test. More waiting, but at least it was only going to be a week or so.

The hospital labs were either very efficient or under a bit less pressure than normal as the results were back on the Tuesday (four working days later). Dr Woods rang me early that evening, just after his surgery was finished.

'Hi Jack, your PSA result is back. It is 5.2. It is a bit higher than we like, but probably nothing to worry about. I think the best thing to do is monitor the situation and do another test in six months to see if there is any change. We will have a more detailed chat when you are down at the surgery in a few weeks.'

Being new to PSA testing, a value of 5.2 didn't really mean a lot but it didn't seem to be too bad. Well, 5.2 is not really a lot above 3 is it?

After this I became more aware of getting up through the night in the sense that I always checked the time and kept a mental count. Waterworks issues were no longer at the fringes of my imagination, they leapfrogged to join the list of things I thought about a lot. It seemed to have this effect on Jane too. Although she usually seemed asleep when I got up, she could always tell me in the morning how many times it had happened and often the times that I had leapt out of the marital bed.

The weeks and months passed.

Six months later I got an email from the surgery asking me to make an appointment with the nurse to get my bloods taken for the agreed follow-up PSA test. All very straightforward. Again Dr Woods rang me when the results came in. My PSA was 9.4 now. He exuded reassurance, more than could be said for me when I heard its value.

'Jack, don't read too much into this. An elevated PSA can occur for many reasons; an enlarged prostate due to benign enlargement, even strenuous exercise, and you would expect it to be a bit higher now you are approaching sixty. Why don't you make an appointment to see me and we can chat through the options? Almost certainly there is a benign reason for this increase.'

Hopefully he was right. Nonetheless, the PSA value *is* meant to be 3 or less – 9.4 certainly is well beyond that! And it was interesting that when he listed a few reasons for an elevated PSA, he didn't mention cancer. Is the word even taboo for most doctors or was he just keeping the positive spin going? Time would tell.

When I contacted the surgery reception to make the appointment, I got speaking to Sonia. She has been the receptionist for so long she seemed more like an office manager and she probably kept the doctors right about so many admin matters. She would be very hard to replace; professional, discreet and always pleasant – nothing was ever too much. Sonia suggested fitting me in at the end of the surgery list the next day as she thought Dr Woods might want to have a longer session than normal with me. Evidence of excellent intra-practice communication, or perhaps she was telepathic. That wouldn't surprise me.

Jane came with me to the appointment. Just for the company on the way, she didn't intend sitting in. There was only a very slight delay. Ten minutes, not too bad for being at the end of the list. Dr Woods was as welcoming as ever. He didn't hang around, he probably wanted to get home for his tea.

'Jack, before we discuss the PSA test, perhaps I should do a physical examination of the prostate.'

I hadn't anticipated this at all. Maybe the short notice was a good thing – I didn't have any time to panic or get anxious, and anyway I wasn't really sure what it involved. But I could work out it was going to be fairly up-close and personal – just glad it wasn't one of the female doctors!

'Lie on the couch, on your side, facing the wall. Lower your trousers to your knees and pull your knees up to your chest. The prostate is just in front of the rectum so I'll be able to examine it coming from the back. You will not feel very much.'

It was over in a flash – the lubricated, gloved finger was inserted, removed, and the glove dispatched to the bin all with one continuous sweep of the arm. I was now familiar with the dreaded DRE (digital rectal examination). Getting down from the couch in a mesmeric state, I got my clothes organised and returned to my seat waiting for the verdict. I wasn't sure whether the cold sweat was due to what I had just gone through or what I might hear.

'All seems fine, there were no obvious irregularities or lumps so it is pretty unlikely you have cancer. However, with your raised PSA we really should make a referral – it would be in the City Hospital. But I must warn you that a prostate biopsy is a pretty unpleasant experience. It doesn't always give the full picture and it can have side effects and there is a fair chance of an infection. Nonetheless, the PSA is nudging up and it's better to have it checked. I would imagine the Consultant will suggest you have a biopsy but you can discuss all this with him.'

I looked on as the letter was dictated into some sort of recording device – in the old days it was called a 'dictaphone'

– who knows what they are known as now, maybe they are still called that – a rare example of technology standing still perhaps.

'It could take a couple of months for them to contact you, as with your PSA score you will not be classified as urgent.'

Progress anyway.

Chapter 5

Gail had slept well, she normally did after going on a five mile run the evening before. Running tired her out but also lifted her mood – it tended to put things in perspective. But she had woken with a slightly sore ankle. And she knew exactly how it had happened. She had slipped on the wet manhole cover she landed on when trying to avoid that idiot who suddenly moved into her path. He obviously had been so dozy (or drunk) he didn't notice that lampstand until very late. Her ankle wasn't that bad that she needed to take the day off, but it was hardly going to improve being on her feet all day in the radiotherapy suite.

After a quick shower, breakfast on the hoof (it was only herself this morning; Steve was starting later – the privilege of the D. Phil. student), it was time to check the backpack. It was the same red backpack Gail had used as a student. She checked the ever-present things; yep, the raincoat was there, the magazine she hadn't got round to reading yet was still there – not that there was likely to be much time for reading at work; her sunglasses too – not that they were likely to be used in December, and her empty one litre water bottle. Empty as the ice cold water in the Cancer Centre drinking fountains was much more refreshing than the water in the flat. To all this she only had to add her small lunch box.

She just had to decide on her footwear. Comfort or fashion, that was the choice. The radiographer uniform is exactly that – uniform by name and uniform in absence of variety. The white overtop with 'registered radiographer' in greeny-blue above the left pocket was the standard attire above navy trousers and trainers. All the radiographers (mainly females, and mainly young females – girls even) wore trendy trainers. They were more comfortable than shoes, but they also had to *look* well, and certainly not showing signs of wear. On this particular morning, Gail chose comfort in favour of fashion. She opted for the *Nike* pair with the extra ankle support.

The overnight rain had stopped so the raincoat remained in the backpack. Gail grabbed her gilet and put that on as she headed for work.

She wasn't due to start until 8.30 but liked to be early. The ten minute walk would get her there by 8.15. She also hoped she might be able to walk off the soreness and stiffness in her ankle. On the way she met up with an old university friend, Tanya, also going to the City Hospital. Tanya had studied diagnostic radiography. She usually worked in the X-ray department. The diagnostic radiographers specialised in medical imaging (X-rays, CT and MRI scans and the like), identifying broken bones and other abnormalities including cancer. Tanya enjoyed this work because she never knew exactly what she was going to find on a particular day – there was always a new type of bone break or a cancer that was growing in a particularly strange way.

Gail had gone down the therapeutic radiography route, she wanted to actually *treat* people. She liked getting to know the patients to some extent – how could you not if you were dealing with them five days a week for up to a couple of months. She was also all too aware that some of the patients, particularly the older ones, had very little human contact in a typical week. Gail was pleased to think that, irrespective of medical outcomes, she did make a difference in the lives of some patients. As her dad used to say, 'it costs nothing to be kind'. As they approached their different destinations, Tanya split first, heading through the Tower Block doors and off to general radiology as Gail continued on into the Cancer Centre. Just short of Christmas, there was a large well-lit Christmas tree in the extensive foyer.

Perhaps an incongruous sign of hope for so many who entered through these doors.

Gail walked into the extensive radiotherapy section in the building, climbed the stairs to the First Floor and abandoned her backpack in the staff quarters. She took her water bottle and filled it on the way to her station – suite number 9. As she passed through the waiting area she could see that about a dozen of the early morning patients had already arrived. Chatting, drinking water (part of the preparation before getting zapped) and generally looking relaxed; for most of the patients you could have been in any type of waiting room; it was the man in the wheelchair and the two ladies without hair that reminded Gail that this was no ordinary waiting area. She recognised a couple of elderly men that were usually treated in her suite, officially called LA9. She liked working in LA9 but was all too aware that she could end up in any of the suites if there was a staff shortage for some of the others. When she checked the staff roster she was pleased to see she was in LA9 together with two of her good friends, Niamh and Toni. Not only were they good friends, they were experienced and competent. They didn't have to be taken through every step as some of the students were – particularly when they were only starting out in their placements.

All good so far, the day was shaping up well.

Chapter 6

The Urology Department appointment was a bit quicker than expected. The letter arrived within five weeks and the appointment was only a couple of weeks after that. It was not an appointment for a biopsy as such, correctly as it turned out, my GP thought that there would be a forerunner appointment to a very probable biopsy further down the line.

My GP, Dr Woods, had warned me that the jury was still out on whether a biopsy was the appropriate response to moderately elevated PSA levels. The procedure was unpleasant at best, with opportunity for infection and other localised damage. Nonetheless, I was looking forward to having this discussion with a specialist. Even if the biopsy showed that there was no cancer, my quality of life was being significantly affected by something (whether bladder, prostate or other malfunction). It would be great to start getting a handle on this and perhaps even alleviating some of the symptoms. They really were bordering on the intolerable.

As expected the appointment was fairly straightforward. The Consultant, Mrs Pawlri, was pleasant, focused and to the point. She could ask a question and subsequently assimilate my answer at the same time as jotting down my answer to the previous question.

Symptoms were discussed in detail; an IPSS form had been completed in the waiting area just before the appointment. The IPSS is an eight part questionnaire that quickly gives clinicians an indication of the severity of prostate problems – usually attributed to prostate enlargement. Seven of the questions ask about the severity of symptoms on a 0 – 5 basis; 0 meaning not affected and 5 meaning affected 'almost always'. Symptoms such 'a sensation of not emptying the bladder fully', 'frequency', 'urgency', and 'number of times being up at the toilet during the night' were included. The maximum score was 35 (a score of 5 in all 7 categories). The scores were added together and then graded: 0-7 was mild; 8-19 was moderate and 20-35 was severe. I came in at 29. The eighth question was a quality of life question. In other words, how important was it for me to do something about alleviating the symptoms. 29 was only one less than my original score of 30 when I first did the test. I suppose all the similarity meant was that the scores could be taken as fairly reliable.

Mrs Pawlri explained that the IPSS was an effective 'ready reckoner' for assessing the state of the problem. It was particularly effective for benign prostatic hyperplasia (BPH), benign (non-cancerous) enlargement of the prostate, a condition that is not particularly dangerous in its own right but can harm the quality of life. The pressure of an enlarged prostate pressing hard on the urethra is going to cause all sorts of problems and could contribute to, or cause, the symptoms listed in the IPSS.

She said, 'based on your feedback, your symptoms are quite severe and are causing you a lot of discomfort. Your quality of life is obviously compromised and you have made it clear that you would prefer to have at least some of the symptoms reduced or stopped. Based on what you are saying, I would recommend that you come in for a biopsy. It is called a trans-rectal ultrasound (TRUS) guided prostate biopsy. The procedure will do two main things; the ultrasound probe will let us have a look at the prostate – it is probably enlarged and this may be due to benign enlargement, a fairly common condition in older men. It will also allow us to take some tissue samples to check for the presence of cancer. At this stage it is impossible to say if any cancerous growth is present. But it is important to stress that most biopsies do not show the presence of cancer.'

I couldn't disagree that this was the best way forward but I did have a few questions myself.

'The procedure is quite unpleasant I've heard, and it can have some nasty side effects.'

'Yes Mr Steenson, it is not particularly pleasant. It tends to cause discomfort rather than actual pain and there is a reasonable chance that you could get an infection or pass blood in your urine for a period. The probe is passed up the rectum and the biopsy needles penetrate the rectal wall to get at the prostate, which lies just in front of the rectum. The doctor performing the biopsy will be able to 'see' the prostate using ultrasound and this is how he or she knows where to take the tissue samples from. It is the penetration of the rectal wall that can lead to unpleasant infections. For this reason we will give you strong antibiotics as part of the process. It is important that you bring someone with you to drive you home. You are likely to be a bit fragile for a time after the procedure.'

After a short discussion about the view out of the Third Floor window, Mrs Pawlri gave me a couple of leaflets on TRUS biopsies. She thought the biopsy was likely to take place in a month or so, although with Christmas looming it could be pushed into early or mid-January.

True to her word, the biopsy was arranged for Thursday 10th January. More literature arrived with the appointment letter. Thankfully the run-up to Christmas would put thoughts of the biopsy out of my head. It did to a large extent, I didn't even bother to look up TRUS biopsy on the Internet. There was nothing that couldn't wait, there were too many nice things to do over Christmas.

But Thursday 10th January did eventually arrive. That morning

I did have a last look over the letter, clocking the advice about not taking valuables if possible. Not a problem, Jane was coming too so she could look after them. I was allowed to have breakfast as normal, but not surprisingly was not particularly hungry. A ripe banana and a cup of very strong coffee did the trick.

Having been to the Urology Department before, it was straightforward getting there this time. I handed in my appointment letter to the same receptionist as on my previous visit, then took a seat in the waiting area waiting for further advice. It was not long in coming. One of the nurses, she introduced herself as Mary, said they would be ready for me in ten minutes. She also said that the whole procedure would take about two hours and that if Jane wanted to disappear to the shops that would be fine as there was not much she could do here within that time. Jane jumped at the chance. The shops were within walking distance, and two hours reading her *Kindle* might just start to drag a bit.

As Jane disappeared through the door out of the department I passed through the curtains into a changing area. One of the nurses came to check my details; DOB, address etc – they certainly were making sure they didn't biopsy the wrong person. I was talked through the procedure, given my antibiotics to take home and left with a gown. The instructions were to wear the gown back to front, open at the back, and to keep my shoes and socks on. As all this was taking place I was able to hear another nurse talking to the elderly man – he must have been at least 75 – in the next bay. Based on his questions, and his answers, he seemed to have little idea of what he was about to go through; perhaps he was the lucky one.

Just before the action the doctor performing the biopsy came for a brief chat. He was a Consultant, but not one I'd met before. At this stage I had to complete the disclaimer form. Five minutes after he disappeared, another nurse (another new one) arrived to bring me through to the 'biopsy' room.

Walking through the door I was greeted by the Consultant, a nurse and an auxiliary nurse. The Consultant asked me to get up on the bed and lie on my side facing the wall (away from him) – I'd been here before! Again, I had to pull my knees up close to my chest. I was given an intravenous antibiotic and there was a bit of chit chat presumably to get me relaxed. The auxiliary nurse squeezed in between me and the wall and started chatting to me. Her role seemed to be to keep me occupied so that I wasn't worrying too much about what was taking place behind me. We soon found out that we had a few things in common. She asked what I did for relaxation and running was one of my answers.

'My husband used to run a lot, he has done the London marathon and a number of half-marathons.'

'Did he ever do the Great North Run on Tyneside?'

'Yes, he did that a couple of times but his last one was the year that a number of people died, I think that was about five years ago.'

This gave me an opportunity to explain that I had done the run the previous September. We chatted about other bits and pieces and as we were talking the Consultant was doing his job.

I didn't actually see the ultrasound probe (I could see the computer monitor where the image would appear) but it would seem that it is ideally shaped for its function. Some internet sources say that a condom is placed over the top of it to help its entry into the body, but it was impossible for me to confirm this. But I did feel it making an entrance. Not sore, but a strange sensation. I had been warned that the spring-loaded needles that would take the prostate tissue samples would sting as they were shot through into the prostate. They did and they went off with some crack – the noise was as bad as the pain. Very similar to an upholstery stapler in sound, I thought later. And of course, the needles were not all fired at once. It seemed as if a couple of needles would shoot into the prostate and then just enough time would elapse to start getting comfortable then off it would go again. I think this was because he was using the probe to target different parts of the prostate. By the time all twelve or so samples had been taken I had had enough. It seemed to last for ages, but in reality was probably less than ten minutes.

The probe seemed to disappear as when I was able to straighten myself up and ease myself off the bed, it was not to be seen. The auxiliary nurse was still chatting away as the other nurse wheeled the trolley containing the monitor (and no doubt the probe) away from the couch. Sliding down the side of the couch onto my feet I certainly was feeling a bit fragile – I could understand why someone needs to be there to drive you home.

The Consultant, Mr Dhani, said that the ultrasound had given him a good look at the prostate and there was some important feedback at this stage.

'Your prostate is about twice the size it should be. Based on what I could see there is almost certainly benign enlargement. This is a good sign, as this enlargement on its own could be causing the increase in PSA level. If the prostate had been normal size we could have ruled out benign enlargement and therefore we might have been looking at something more dangerous. We cannot rule out cancer, of course, until we get results back from the labs, but that is less likely now. The very large prostate can explain why you have so many symptoms. We will give you some medication that will help shrink the prostate. It will take time, weeks or even months though before some of your symptoms are a lot better.'

The auxiliary nurse, Orla, walked me the short distance back to the changing area. Tea and biscuits were organised and the tea was so welcome I finished it before I got changed. I was reminded that I couldn't leave until I had been to the loo, just to check that the waterworks were still functioning. And I had to pee into a see-through plastic jug when the time came. I assume so that they could check just how much blood was present in the urine. By the time I was dressed, the tea had had its effect. I walked gingerly to the loo and was able to produce a straw coloured sample. Difficult to say if there was any blood there. Just before leaving, one of the nurses gave me the prescription for *Combodart,* the drug used to start reducing the size of the prostate that the Consultant had referred to.

By the time I left the department, just over an hour and a half after I had arrived, Jane was sitting waiting for me. I was glad to see her. I suggested going for a coffee in town but Jane proposed that we go home and get a coffee there. It would be more restful, she said. And of course she was right.

Chapter 7

I picked up the *Combodart* from the pharmacy the following day. There was no reason to wait. As the pharmacist prepared the prescription I could see her lifting my *Combodart* box from its own neat pile on the shelf. There seemed to be no shortage of them – I certainly wasn't on my own going through this.

Having brought the tablets home, Jane then had a quick look through the patient advice leaflet. I wasn't sure whether she was just interested in how it would work or was really having a look at the side effects. Either way, she seemed pretty interested in it.

It was a few days later that she casually, very casually, raised the topic of *Combodart* over breakfast.

'Jack, have you had a look through the patient leaflet that comes with the *Combodart*?'

'No, but I'll have a look after breakfast. It does say that it is for an enlarged prostate, doesn't it, I mean I have the right stuff?'

'Oh yeah, you have the right stuff OK. It will probably shrink your prostate. You will get better sleep I would imagine, but it might come at a price. Possibly a very high price.'

Somewhere at the back of my mind I could remember some discussion about the medication for an enlarged prostate – reduced sexual drive seemed to spring to mind as a common side effect.

'No I haven't had a look at the side effects, but fill me in. What can I expect?'

'No, read the leaflet yourself and we can have a chat later. But it's no big deal.'

Once breakfast was over I dug the leaflet out as Jane filled the dishwasher. The information was clear, easy to read and in relatively straightforward language – another victory for the plain English brigade.

'Jane, have you noticed that some of the side effects can be very common – over a 10% chance of being affected?'

'Yes, and have you read what they are Jack?'

'I'm afraid so, impotence, decreased sex drive blah, blah. When we get to our age we need all the help we can get, we don't need obstacles in that department.'

I wasn't really sure how Jane was going to take all this. I wasn't really sure how I was going to feel about all this myself. But Jane was great.

'Don't worry Jack, we'll take it as it comes and if you get those side effects so be it. It is not a problem.'

Nor was it. But what if it had been? I didn't want to think. The tablets were obviously very potent. At the start they were making me a bit dizzy. It was a few weeks later that the letter from the hospital arrived. It was clear that it was a copy of the letter that had been sent to my GP. And as expected it confirmed was the consultant had thought.

'This gentleman has had a TRUS biopsy of the prostate. The biopsy did not show evidence of malignancy. There was a small amount of prostatic intraepithelial neoplasia. His IPSS score is 30 and he is currently on Combodart.

I have arranged flow rate investigations and a bladder scan.'

Most of this made sense but I wasn't sure about the *prostatic intraepithelial neoplasia*. A quick internet search told me that this was evidence of abnormal cells in the prostate. Not cancer certainly, but in some cases a pre-cancerous condition. I took the *'small amount'* to be significant. It seemed that very few older men had totally normal prostates. This didn't seem to be significant, otherwise they would want to see me. Wouldn't they?

When I saw Dr Woods a few weeks later he wasn't too worried about the degree of abnormality present. I heard again that famous phrase, 'most men die with prostate cancer, not because of it.'

Anyhow a few weeks later I received an appointment for the flow rate test. It was described as a 'nurse-led' investigation. Assumed that all this meant was that I wouldn't be seeing the Consultant.

••••

Meanwhile, Gail was getting on great. In her third year in the Cancer Centre she was loving her job. Getting up in the morning was easier when you enjoyed how you spent your day. There was also a real buzz between her and Steve. Maybe he would be the one. Too early to say, but possible. Certainly a lot better than that last prat, even thinking about Fred made her shiver. What had she ever seen in him?

Steve would obviously do well, he was so bright and so well qualified. All those letters and all those papers with his name at the top. But Gail was part of that generation where things didn't always fall into place. There just weren't enough jobs. You could have a D. Phil. and end up stacking shelves in *Tesco* – ridiculous but true. But last night's conversation did make her think a bit. It wasn't hard to retrace it in her mind.

'Gail, I know you love your job but I don't know an awful lot about the career progression. Someone like you should be rocketing up the scale and be in management before too long. What actually is a typical progression path? Is there one?'

'That maybe is the downside, Steve. There are not really a lot of opportunities to progress. But that is not the only thing. With the ridiculous idea to delay the retirement age to sixty five or even longer, what will I be like moving patients on the couch when I'm sixty? Some of them are hard enough to move now. Anyhow, I have noticed that there are not too many radiotherapists over forty, I suspect that many of them throw their cap at the young doctors and get married off. If only!'

'Yeah Gail, you needn't worry about all this now. Far too many years away. Who knows what will happen by then? Climate change will finish us off, or something else – look at the state of the Middle East – the whole world's in turmoil. Sixty is light-years away.'

••••

The flow test was straightforward. There seemed to be a small room – annex more like – dedicated for this function in the Urology Department. You simply had to pee into a specially adapted sink-like structure and the rate of flow or force was measured in some way. To ensure the test could take place the nurses had given me a large drink of water beforehand. All was clearly well. The sink seemed to be made of aluminium and I could have been listening to a hail shower on a tin roof. No problems there.

The bladder scan was completed immediately after the flow rate test. It was a bit more restful, so much so that I could almost have dosed off. Lying on top of the couch the nurse passed an ultrasound probe over my abdomen. All seemed fine.

And that was that. The waterworks could take a back seat for a while. The next thing on the agenda was another PSA test and an appointment in Urology in about a year's time. Time to start focusing on work and the nice things in life.

Chapter 8

The follow-up appointment was the next September, just a bit under a year from the first biopsy. Usual format and another new Consultant's name on the letter. Another PSA test to be taken in advance. Working backwards, there was not much time from between getting the letter and needing to get my bloods taken. That is if I was going to have my PSA in time for the appointment.

In due course that was all sorted. The PSA was 11.2. Certainly higher than hoped and not really what was expected. The plan had been that the *Combodart* would shrink the prostate to something approaching normal size. A shrinking prostate should mean a shrinking PSA value, shouldn't it? It left me a bit confused but I was going to the right place to have it explained.

I've always been a supporter of the NHS. Perhaps I've been lucky. But there were too many examples of good practice and kindness beyond the immediate confines of duty to have any other view. Epitomised by the phone call from the surgery. It wasn't Dr Woods, he was on holiday. It was Dr Phillips, a young locum who I had only seen once before. She rang me to tell me my PSA score was 11.2, obviously not knowing that I had already contacted the surgery to find this out. She was keen to get me in for an appointment with her to discuss the next step. She clearly didn't know I was to have an appointment with a Urology Consultant the following week. Dr Phillips was pleased to hear that and wished me well.

September was a pretty good month. Sweet pea and the roses were in full bloom. Cutting the grass was good aerobic exercise and lifted the spirits. The garden needed watering most days, not many summers you could say that this far north. Jane was busy, she had a number of translations to be done in her in-tray. But nothing that couldn't wait if we could get a cheapie to Majorca.

In the end we didn't go. The weather was just too good here.

An advantage was that I could keep my appointment at the City. If we had gone to Majorca I might have had to postpone it for a few weeks. So September 8th remained the date – it was for the Urology Clinic, although this time it was based in the main Outpatients complex. Finding the clinic was not a problem and the appointment was on time. The explanation of the raised PSA was all that was needed I thought.

Mr Evans was very pleasant. He ran me through my current symptoms and checked my medication. It was when he checked my mediation list that he started to become a bit more focused and concentrated. I could sense that he was twigging on to something.

'When exactly did you start the *Combodart,* Jack?

'After the biopsy, last January or so.'

'This puts a different complexion on the PSA score. If you are on *Combodart*, we have to double your score to give an effective PSA reading. This means your PSA is really around 20. In terms of diagnosis this is a very different proposition to having a score of around 11. I really think you need another biopsy to check this out. You are a relatively young man to have prostate problems so we really need to get this sorted.'

He was quietly spoken but it wasn't hard to get his drift.

'Dr Evans, will I have long to wait for the biopsy?'

'No, around a month is all it will take. As a tertiary centre we have good capacity here.'

I had to ask the obvious question, 'do you think it is likely it is prostate cancer?'

'It is possible, but we cannot be sure. If you have already had a biopsy a year or so ago, statistically there is less chance of finding cancer in this one than there was in the first biopsy. Of course as you know, the first biopsy could have missed cancer in its early stages. And of course, so could this one, but it is fairly unlikely two biopsies will miss it should it be there. Better to make sure. You will get a letter in a couple of weeks or so giving you the date. And you do know what the biopsy is like, which helps. It is not a particularly pleasant procedure, is it?'

The answer was so obvious it barely needed to be made. True to his word, the letter arrived a couple of weeks later. When it arrived I photocopied it as I did them all. The photocopied pile in my bedside drawer was growing almost by the week.

Jane also knew the score. Once we got the date she blanked out the whole day in her diary. She knew that I wouldn't be fit for much after the biopsy. We didn't talk about it until the drive into town.

'Are you worried about this Jack?'

'Not in the sense of what they will find. I'm not looking forward to the procedure, it stings like hell.'

'The joys of getting old Jack. At least we still have our marbles.'

I had driven in. We were only able to find a parking space on the top floor of the multi-storey park – that is the penalty for having an appointment mid-morning. The early shift get the best places. I reversed in to make it as easy as I could for Jane to drive out when the time for home came.

The Urology waiting area was busy. Much more so than when I'd been before. There must have been more going on than biopsies. A short time later I was called in to the changing area. Jane wasn't going shopping on this occasion. She had brought her *Kindle* and a paper. She said she might nip down to the hospital canteen for a coffee, but that was as far as she was going. It all seemed so familiar. The same nurse as the first time brought me my gown and explained the procedure. After sitting twenty minutes or so I was starting to feel the cold. The gown preserved dignity but not heat. I wasn't completely sure whether the shivering was totally due to the cold or whether I was a bit nervous. Maybe I did remember the procedure all too well.

After what seemed like ages, the 'Consultant' came through with her consent forms. She was in her green scrubs and crocs and seemed to be in her thirties. She explained that she was in fact a Registrar rather than a Consultant. It hardly mattered, it is not as if the procedure itself is particularly complicated. The nurse informed her that this was my second time. That pleased her. No need to explain the whole ritual. This would quicken things up. Get the morning back on track. After signing the form she said she would send for me in about five minutes. Great, that means it would all be over in about twenty minutes. All over bar the pain that is. And all over bar the wait for the results, that was probably going to be the worst bit.

Entering the procedure room a few minutes later, it all came flashing back. The same room, the same equipment, the same auxiliary nurse. I think she remembered me, as she seemed to start chatting where we had left off before. As before, she squeezed herself into the tiny space between the couch and the wall. Then off we went. The Registrar and the nurse at the business-end pulled down their face visors and got me into exactly the position they wanted.

'I'll just do a quick examination before we start the biopsy Jack. It'll only take a few seconds. After that you will the feel the probe entering but I'll let you know before we start taking samples. You will remember the sting and the noise I'm sure from the first time.'

'Too right, doctor. But the sooner we get started the sooner it will be over.'

The next ten minutes were no more pleasant than the first time. Possibly even worse.

When the procedure was completed, I raised myself up from lying on my side, tied up the gown and took a few minutes to settle myself before sliding off the couch. If I had any questions now was the time.

'How did the prostate feel, are you able to give me any feedback at this stage?'

'I think it is better to wait until we get the biopsy results back as it is not really possible to say for sure,' she replied in a non-commital way. 'Your prostate certainly has reduced in size and that will be the effect of the *Combodart*. You probably are finding it easier to pee, now that you don't have an enlarged prostate pressing on the urethra.'

'A bit, but the main issue is the fact that I get very little warning when I need to run to the toilet. Urgency, is how you describe it I think.'

'OK, I'll write you a prescription for medication that will make your bladder more relaxed, I think that is what is causing this problem. Your bladder has had to work very hard to force the urine through the restricted urethra when the prostate was enlarged so that its muscles are now damaged and are unable to work in a more gentle and controlled way.'

Back in the changing area the tea and biscuits were as welcome as before. As before, I couldn't go until I had produced a sample in one of the plastic jugs in the adjacent loo. I didn't have to wait too long and while there was clearly some blood present, there didn't seem to be a lot.

Antibiotics in my pocket, I then went back into the waiting area to meet Jane.

I wasn't great the next few days, more blood in the urine and I definitely felt a bit off. Possibly an infection from the biopsy.

However, it did clear within a few days, as did the blood in the urine. Now all there was to do was wait for the results. I didn't know why but I felt a bit less confident than I had done after the first biopsy.

Chapter 9

Some would say it was the letter that changed everything. Those classic sentences '*This appointment will give you an opportunity to discuss details with the Consultant. A friend or relative is welcome to accompany you*' were really a giveaway in retrospect. Was there really any doubt?

The letter, hearing the diagnosis with the specialist oncology nurse sitting in the background, all seemed light years away now. A further appointment with Mr Jackson was made for the middle of January. They were certainly giving me enough time to get used to the diagnosis. I didn't need time, what I needed was action. Treatment.

Christmas came and went. It was fairly relaxed and cancer was rarely thought about and barely mentioned. I had just blocked it all out. I didn't even want to start thinking about whether the cancer had spread or not and what the treatment would involve. As the Christmas holidays came to an end and postal services returned to something approaching normal, in the brief period between the Christmas and New Year holidays, there was another hospital letter. This was an appointment letter for an MRI scan in early January. Written in on pen was an additional appointment for an isotope bone scan on the same day. Planning the two scans a few hours apart on the same day was good news and showed consideration as well as organisation. There was enough detail to work out that the MRI scan was for the pelvic region, no doubt to give further information re the exact size and site of the tumour. The other scan was a whole body bone scan to check if the cancer had spread to the bones, a likely outcome if the primary had metastasised. Hopefully that one would be clear, if it had reached the bone, things were going to be much more complicated.

The scans were on the first Tuesday after the New Year, the day after the schools went back. The traffic would also be back to normal. Still it would be easier and more comfortable to take the car. The good news was that the first scan was not until 10 in the morning so I would miss the worst of the traffic. I was starting to become familiar with the route, particularly the lane layout at the Broadway roundabout, the only difficult section of the whole journey. There was plenty of space in the high rise car park, which was a bit of a surprise. Perhaps, things were not fully up and running in the New Year as yet.

Both scans were to take place in the Cancer Centre. I think this was to be my first time in the building. The revolving doors opened into an extensive foyer with a coffee shop on the left and a large reception desk in the centre. Lifts and stairs were to the left and the entrances to Radiotherapy and Radiology were on the right. Two semi-circular rows of soft seats were sited midway between the reception desk and the side walls, one row on each side facing inwards. The place was bright and there was a positive atmosphere, a real sense of purpose. Most of the seats were occupied, impossible to say whether by patients or relatives accompanying patients.

I had to check the letter again to see if my appointments were in Radiology or Radiotherapy. The distinction is obvious once you know the difference but I, like many others I'm sure, wasn't entirely confident of the difference on my first visit.

Radiology it was. Straight through the doors on the right beamed the receptionist. The Radiology reception was down the corridor on the right and the receptionist there took my details and shepherded me further down the corridor to the MRI suite. Details were again checked. Plenty of form filling in this business. When the radiographer was sure they had the right person I was given a gown and taken to a cubicle to get changed.

The radiographers were reassuring, emphasising that there was nothing to worry about and checking that I wasn't claustrophobic, not that they could probably do much if I was. There would be a strange clunking noise as the scanning was taking place I was told. It didn't really last very long but they were able to tell me they were doing both a detailed scan of the prostate and a more general one of the wider pelvic area.

After the MRI scan I had time to nip to the shop in the centre for a quick coffee before returning for the bone scan. The bone isotope suite was in a different part of the Radiology Department. It seemed to be a bit less busy and the medical staff appeared to double up as receptionists. Eventually I was scooped up by the scan operator. I think he was a specialised medical physicist rather than a bespoke radiologist. He took me through the process. I was to take a drink containing a radioisotope substance and disappear for a couple of hours for the radioisotope to get into my system. He explained that as blood (containing the isotope) will be channelled to the more metabolically active parts of the body it is likely to target actively growing regions such as clumps of cancer cells. During the scan, actively growing regions would show up as 'hot spots' as there will be a greater concentration of isotope in these regions.

Before leaving he told me exactly where to return to and at exactly what time. More coffee – the intention was to flush out the excess radioisotope. Not that the isotope would do me too much harm as it would be excreted fairly quickly anyway. The problem was that if there was too much excess isotope swirling around in my circulation it may mask any small contrast in my skeleton.

The bone scan was less noisy and less claustrophobic than the earlier MRI scan. Lying on my back the couch slowly moved into and out of the machine bringing the prostrate me with it.

Again it didn't take too long. I was hoping to get some feedback on what it had shown up before I departed but I was out of luck on that one. It was only as I left the building that I really took on board the importance of a positive outcome to that scan. The last thing I needed were 'hot spots' anywhere in my bones.

Jane had the coffee ready by the time I got home but I had had more than enough caffeine. My head was buzzing. And I realised it was due to more than the caffeine; I really had to get the significance of the bone scan out of my head for now.

I did have a scone as I filled Jane in with the details of my double date in radiology. As we were chatting I spotted my post on the table. Most of it was the usual junk but the hospital letter was easy to spot. Jane did well not to open it while I was away for so long. The format of the letter was familiar so I quickly skipped to the business part. I had an appointment the following week with a Clinical Oncologist in the Cancer Centre. This was a bit out of the blue as I thought my next appointment was to be in Urology in about two weeks' time. Seemed also a bit strange as the results from the scans may not be available? Perhaps they would be and the whole process was a bit more joined up than I thought. Time would tell.

Chapter 10

Gail spent her week off at Christmas up on the North Coast with her mother and brother. It was also an opportunity to spend time with old school friends. Many had remained locally and most of those who had travelled further afield came home for the festivities. Steve had gone to visit his parents and his young brother who was still living at home.

It was a welcome break from work. The radiotherapy suites were working to capacity. Not surprising as the Cancer Centre was a Centre of Excellence for radiotherapy. While there was talk that a new radiotherapy centre would be built on the North Coast it was certainly not ready yet. Gail wasn't even sure if it was definitely going to happen with all the cutbacks. There seemed to be no end to these, although they didn't seem to be directly affecting her job too much, not as yet anyway.

Gail's mother had settled into a routine since the death of her husband Brian. She had adapted well to the change in routine over the last few years. She could do many of the 'man' tasks he used to do; cutting the grass, ordering the central heating oil, taking the car for its service, catching the spiders. It was Gail or her brother's job to do much of the rest.

Gail loved beachcombing. She was into nature in a big way. Most mornings she would leave the semi-detached house she was brought up in close to Magilligan Strand and go down to the shore. Some mornings she had her running gear on and would run a couple of miles along the shore, really enjoying her smooth running rhythm on the sand. The little bit of give in the sand was a welcome change from running on Belfast's concrete pavements; she also knew it was better for her knees. Other mornings she would just walk along the shore, marvelling at the superb scenery so close to her home, and in a world of her own, looking for anything new that had drifted in during the night.

The break from the routine of work was great. Much as she liked her work, positioning thirty to forty patients each day and then checking their treatment on the monitor could be fairly mind-numbing, particularly if there wasn't much chat out of them. Mind you, the variety was interesting. Some patients were totally up to speed on their treatment; their chances, the probable side effects, and others just didn't have a clue; they might as well be at the dentists. You met all life in this job. But in the main it was positive.

She felt particularly sorry for those getting palliative treatment, particularly if it appeared that they had just let things drift until it was too late. And this was all too frequent. It wasn't that there was a negative correlation between the intelligence of the patient and the speed of diagnosis; it was clear some very bright people too had a blank when it came to their own health. Particularly men. And particularly prostate patients, she surmised. It was very sad to see many of the patients with advanced disease struggling down the corridors on their walking sticks, crutches or zimmers. The outcome for many of these patients was all too clear to see. She knew she couldn't dwell on it if she was going to survive as a radiotherapist.

She couldn't help but think about her dad; why had he left it so late? He was bright, he should have known. Sometimes it was all too much for Gail. She just felt so guilty. Why could he not have been saved, like many of the patients she worked with every day. The unfairness of life niggled at her. While her mother was coping with day to day tasks, she was not the same person she was before Brian had died. Gail's father had died but it was her mother who had lost her spirit. Gail came home as often as she could, this helped but she wished she could do something that would really make a difference. She was determined to bring Steve up the next time she returned home. She thought this might help her mother. Something positive to focus on rather than thinking about the past. Let's just hope her relationship with Steve doesn't go pear shaped, she thought, but she had the feeling it wouldn't. That thought put a spring in her step as she glided along in the sand.

Gail could see what was needed, her mother had to move on. And so did she, if she really thought about it. But she was bright enough to know that understanding the problem was different to being able to do something about it.

Chapter 11

A quick internet search told me exactly what an oncologist was. I knew they were 'cancer docs' of some form or other. It seems they are specialist doctors who treat cancer by non-surgical methods; I assumed this mainly means chemotherapy and radiotherapy.

I caught the train on the day I was scheduled to see Dr Gavasker. The appointment was on the First Floor of the Cancer Centre. I arrived about 20 minutes early. It's hard to get old habits out of the system, I really hate the stress of arriving late for anything. The waiting area was awash with *Macmillan* leaflets and other cancer care brochures. There were about ten others in the waiting area when I arrived. Two or three of them were young women, probably in their early twenties. They were all totally relaxed and showed no signs of panic or anxiety. The positive atmosphere I first experienced on the Ground Floor when I arrived for my scans appeared to extend throughout the entire building. Part of the reason I'm sure was the fact that the building is relatively new, no dusty and dark corners or cracked walls. This place certainly didn't give the impression that the NHS was under financial pressure, or on its knees. Maybe cancer care was under less pressure that other less fashionable areas such as mental health? Cancer care is certainly more politically sensitive and the politicians need to please the masses.

Upon arrival, the receptionist had given me a disk that would light up when my appointment was to take place. On time, the disk started flashing and simultaneously, a doctor, I assumed Dr Gavasker, appeared at the corridor entrance to the interview suites. She took my flashing disk and returned it to the reception. She explained that the introduction of the flashing disk system was to allow patients to be in any part of the Cancer Centre (e.g. the loo or even the coffee shop on the Ground Floor) and they could be alerted to the fact that their appointment was due.

Dr Gavasker was probably in her late thirties or early forties based on appearance. Glad to say, she seemed on the ball, she seemed to know exactly what was going on. After the inevitable pleasantries we got down to the matter in hand.

'We have got your results back from the scans. The bone scan has confirmed that the cancer has not spread to your bones as yet, which is good news. The MRI scan shows us that the tumour extends right across the prostate gland and it is pushing on the external capsule. I think at this stage it is too late for surgery and radiotherapy is the option I'm advising. Perhaps the only real option at this stage.'

That was a bit of a shock. Dr Jackson in Urology had suggested that either surgery or radiotherapy were options.

'Dr Gavasker, why does it have to be radiotherapy?'

'You have what is described as locally advanced prostate cancer. There is a significant chance that the cancer has escaped from the prostate. The biopsy showed that there was perineural invasion with the cancer tracking the nerve to the edge of the prostate. While the MRI scan did not pick up cancer beyond the prostate, we have to bear in mind that the scan will not pick up small clumps of cells that are smaller than a few millimetres. There is a genuine risk that the cancer has spread into the pelvic area, although we cannot say for definite one way or the other. But we have to assume that it might have.'

It really wasn't getting any better.

'Dr Gavasker, I assume we are talking about treatment here? We are assuming that this can be cured?'

'That is what we are hoping, Jack. We had a meeting with the multidisciplinary team last Friday and the pathologist confirmed that your cancer is particularly aggressive. He gave it a Gleason score of 8, which is pretty near the maximum. In reality, this means that the cancer cells divide very rapidly, and therefore, there is an increased risk that they have escaped from the prostate. In other words your cancer may not be organ-confined as I suggested earlier.'

'What really does this mean, we are talking cure, aren't we?' I realised that this was the second time I had asked this. I also realised the importance of a positive answer.

'We are, but we would regard you as high risk.'

'And what does high risk mean, statistically?'

'It means that patients presenting with disease at your stage and aggressiveness have a 70-80% chance of surviving prostate cancer for another five years. I have already said that it has to be radiotherapy, and it has to be external beam radiotherapy, as we have to target the wider pelvic area as well as the prostate itself. Additionally, I would like to start you on hormone therapy as soon as possible. We do this for most of our prostate cancer patients when it is described as locally advanced. The hormone is to stop you producing testosterone which we now know is a driver for prostate cancer. However, before we decide on which hormone therapy to use we need to review the options. We want to balance treatment with quality of life, as far as we possibly can.'

And then it came.

'Jack, are you sexually active?'

This came like a bolt from the blue.

'Theoretically yes, but *Combodart* doesn't do a terrible lot for that department. And I've been on that for the last year or so. I'm not sure that hormone therapy will really make a massive difference on top of the effects of the *Combodart*.'

'There are two ways in which we can suppress the testosterone. You can have monthly, eventually three monthly, injections or take tablets on a more regular basis. As with most options in treating prostate cancer there is a significant risk of side effects. Both the hormone injections and tablets are equally effective, the difference is mainly in the side effects. The hormone injections will almost certainly cause impotence and a reduced libido, whereas these effects are not quite so bad with the tablets; they are still there but not quite so bad. With the injections, hot flushes are very common. However, the tablets can lead to significant breast growth, very significant growth. But at the end of the day it is your choice. I'm not really expecting you to make up your mind today. How long do you think you will need to decide on which hormone option to follow?'

'Just a few days, I would like to discuss this with Jane.'

'OK, we'll make an appointment for this day next week.'

'That's fine, I'm pretty sure it will be the injections but a few days will give me a chance to think about it and talk it through with Jane. Anyhow, when do you think the radiotherapy will start?'

'In about three months. We like patients to have about three months on hormone therapy before we start. Additionally, it takes us around eight weeks to plan your radiotherapy regime. Your planning will be particularly complex as we have to work on the assumption that the cancer may have spread into the pelvic area. The radiotherapy will need to target the wider pelvic area as well as the tumour in the prostate. There is a very fine balance between destroying the tumour and not damaging the healthy cells too much. There are significant side effects with the radiotherapy as well, I'm afraid. But we will discuss these when you are in next week. We have probably covered enough for today. But before you go I'll get the nurse to take some bloods. We will do another PSA test and a few other tests to give us a baseline before the hormone therapy starts.'

'When you come in next week let me know your decision concerning the hormone therapy. In addition, we will take you through the forms and discuss side effects. I'll also ask one of the radiotherapists to come up and discuss the radiotherapy process with you.'

Yes, she was right, it was enough for one day. After going down the stairs to the foyer, I decided not to go straight down to the train halt but nipped into the coffee shop to gather my wits and mentally play back all that had just been said. As always the coffee was beautiful. It hit the right spots. What a strange place to get the best coffee in Belfast.

Chapter 12

Jane picked me up from the station. As always, she was keen to know how I got on but she was happy to wait for me to start the discussion.

'It looks like a combination of hormone therapy and radiotherapy. Cannot be surgery as they think it may have gone beyond the prostate.'

'I thought you were already on hormone therapy, Jack. Is that not what the *Combodart* is?'

'I thought so too but apparently not, or at least not in the sense of the hormone therapy I'm about to start.'

'When is all this going to start?'

'The hormone therapy will start over the next week or so. I have to pick up my prescription when I'm in next week.'

'You have another appointment next week? You are certainly getting your share out of the NHS.'

'Yes, I think that appointment is threefold. I have to let Dr Gavasker know whether I'm going to take the hormone by injections or tablets. The reality is that there are two different families of hormones; they work in different ways and they have different side effects. They both stop testosterone getting to the prostate which is pretty important by all accounts. I will also have a number of forms to sign and I'm going to meet someone from radiotherapy, although the radiotherapy itself will not start for a couple of months.'

'Jack, what are the side effects you are talking about with the hormones?'

'The hormone zaps any sex drive, that is any that is left after the *Combodart*, and causes hot flushes; the tablets cause you to grow breasts but you may have some sex drive left if you are lucky. Great choice.'

'Which option do you think you will go for?'

'I thought the injections, what do you think?'

'Would tend to agree. At least if you are on the injections you will look the same. Man-boobs would be a nightmare, you would look freakish. We can cope with the other. It's not a problem. The important thing is getting you well as soon as possible, that is the priority, Jane said, returning my anxious glance with a smile.

'Anyhow, how are you getting on with the bladder tablets you were prescribed at the time of the biopsy?'

'They seem to be working well in that I can walk as opposed to having to run to the loo. But they have their own side effects as well. I have a very dry mouth a lot of the time. It's probably a matter of trying to work out which is worse. If the dry mouth is more irritating I'll stop the tablets and try to manage the other problem better. It's really 50:50 at the minute, let's see what it is like after I've been on it for longer.'

'You can get special mouthwashes to reduce the effect of the dry mouth. I've seen them in *Boots*. I'll pick you up one when I'm next in. Let's see if that helps. We'll try to nail that before any of the other side effects come cascading in.'

We decided to go out for a meal that Saturday. The second weekend in January is never too busy so we had our pick. We went to a nice Italian in the university area. Once I started the hormone therapy and the radiotherapy, going out might be a bit more complex, particularly having read about the myriad of potential complications both can bring. Everything in its own time.

The second appointment with Dr Gavasker rattled around quickly enough. As before I was given the appointment disk after I signed in, and as before, it started flashing when Dr Gavasker was ready.

Before we could discuss the hormone options she told me that the PSA results were back. It was still 11 point something but as Dr Gavasker reminded me we could effectively double that score due to the effects of the *Combodart*. In her softly-spoken, but authoritative style, she gently reviewed the position: 'effective PSA of around 20, tumour pushing on the edge of the prostate, very aggressive cancer with a Gleason score of 8, perineural invasion. Hormone therapy and radiotherapy, has to be this for a high risk patient such as yourself. Have you come up with a decision about whether you will go for the injections or the tablets? And have you considered the side effects of each?'

'Yes doctor, we are happy enough to go with the injections,' I replied, and then glanced at her face to gauge the response.

'I noticed you used the '*we*' word, which is good. The tablets are a relatively new option; there is much more research available about the effectiveness of the injections, they do work. There is unlikely to be much tumour growth while you are on hormone therapy. The radiotherapy will hopefully destroy the cancer cells that are there. OK, I'll write you a letter for your GP organising your monthly injections. You will also have to get your GP or practice nurse to actually administer the injections. You'll not be able to do them at home.'

'Now we have that sorted and you are aware of the side effects the hormone therapy can, or in reality, will bring, we need to talk through the radiotherapy and the possibility of side effects there. With the radiotherapy, you may get some side effects, you may get none, it is just impossible to say.'

Dr Gavasker read through the list of possible side effects of radiotherapy. Impotence, loss of sex drive, incontinence, noting that some may be temporary and others may be more long lasting. They may occur during treatment or in the months or years after. And of course, if the gods are all on side, I could escape them all. Having been through the list on the consent form, I was reminded that the intention is that radiotherapy will cure the cancer, just in case I was having doubts, before being asked to sign the consent form.

Formalities complete, she phoned down to radiotherapy and asked for one of the radiotherapists to come up and see me, to explain the procedure. Dr Gavasker took me down the corridor to a small room which had a couple of soft chairs, one on either side of a low wooden table. Once I was installed in one of the chairs, she departed to pick up her next patient.

About five minutes later, I could hear the soft squeak of trainer sole on the corridor floor. The owner of those particular trainers glided into the room and before sitting down opposite me began by introducing herself.

'Hello Mr Steenson, I'm Gail from radiotherapy. The Radiotherapy Department is almost directly underneath us on the Ground Floor. You will be coming to us for treatment in six to eight weeks. It might seem a long time but it takes this length of time for your program to be worked out and checked. Dr Gavasker says your program is going to be fairly complex so it is likely to take longer to work out than many do.'

'Have you any questions before I take you through the process.' For someone who seemed so young, Gail seemed to be confident in a way that oozed reassurance. Of course, this was hardly the first time she was explaining radiotherapy to a patient.

'No, just you go ahead and explain what's involved.'

'Once we get everything set up it is all very straightforward, the complexity is in the planning. You will come in for thirty seven consecutive days, excluding weekends and Bank Holidays, and each day you will be given a small dose, or fraction as we call it, of radiation. Your treatment is tailored specifically to meet your needs and the plan is to do as much harm to the cancer cells as possible but to avoid too much damage to your healthy cells. Having the weekend off gives your healthy cells time to recover. You will need to be here for at least an hour before your appointment time to get prepared. For example, if your appointment time is 10.30 you will need to be here by 9.30.'

'What does the preparation involve?'

'It is really about ensuring we reduce the chances of healthy cells being harmed. We ask you to have taken 500 millilitres of water by forty minutes or so before you get your treatment. And that you do not go to the loo between the water loading and the radiotherapy to pass water. It can be difficult but you need to have a very full bladder. A full bladder springs back away from the prostate and this means that there is less chance of the bladder being harmed by the radiation.'

'All makes sense, but what happens if you cannot wait the forty minutes before running to the loo?' I asked, feeling stupid about my inability to hang on and thinking about any number of potential disasters.

'In all probability, we would have to start the process again. Don't worry too much at this stage, most men can manage to wait for their radiotherapy slot. 500 ml is four of those small cups sitting on the sink behind you or a standard small bottle of water. At the start of the preparation you will need to take an enema – I'm sure you have read about this in one of the leaflets you were given.'

'Yes, but I was hoping I might be able to avoid that!'

'I understand, but it is important that your bowel is as empty as possible. If so it becomes a much smaller target and so less likely to be damaged by radiation. Once the preparation is complete, the actual radiotherapy is pretty straightforward. Any questions?'

'Just the one, do I have to take the enema every day?'

'Afraid so, but you will get used to it.'

'Is there any pain or discomfort?'

'There shouldn't be any pain. You will feel nothing during the radiotherapy but holding on to the water is likely to create some discomfort and taking the enema will be unpleasant but hopefully no more than that.'

'Hopefully', I quipped, as Gail smiled at the black humour. The conversation we were having seemed all so unreal. A few months earlier I would never have dreamt that I would be going through all this.

'Before you actually start the radiotherapy we will get you in for a planning scan. This is to check the exact position of the tumour and to get a few reference points on your body so we can line you up properly and make sure we are targeting the correct area. Have you any preferences about the time of the day you would like the treatment to take place? We tend to give you a time slot and ask you to stick to that time throughout the treatment.'

'First thing in the morning would be great, means I can get it over and done with.'

'That's fine, the first appointment is 8.30, but you would need to be in by 7.30 to start your preparation. Is that still OK?'

'Yes, that's fine, I'll go for an 8.30 slot. At that time the traffic should not be too bad and there are unlikely to be long delays.'

'True.'

Gail checked that there was nothing more I needed to know and tried to reassure me by making the point that I was about to go through something that was tried and trusted. We both rose simultaneously and headed for the door seemingly on automatic pilot. We walked together along the corridor and down the stairs to the Ground Floor. As I turned right and left the Cancer Centre through the revolving doors Gail headed back into radiotherapy. I had learned enough to know that the Radiotherapy Department was going to become like a second home over the coming months.

Chapter 13

On the way home from the hospital I dropped my letter from Dr Gavasker into the Health Centre where my GP Dr Woods was based. I had a quick look before handing it in – had it been more complicated I might have been tempted to bring it home to get it photocopied first.

The prescription was for 3 mg *Decapeptyl* which was to be administered by injection. Dr Gavasker's letter made it clear that the injection therapy was to be continued at four-weekly intervals until radiotherapy started. At that stage, depending on side effects, I had the option to move to 11.25 mg every three months.

Further down the letter there was further information for the GP.

'I would appreciate if the patient's cardiovascular risk factors including blood pressure, blood glucose and cholesterol could be assessed 6 monthly, since this hormone therapy has recently been associated with a small increase in cardiovascular and metabolic events.'

'Events' appeared to be an interesting term in this context. Reading this made me make a mental note that I would need to check this up at the next appointment. I needed to know if I was at increased risk of a stroke or a heart attack. More to worry about.

Driving home from the surgery I quickly worked out what I still had to do. Tomorrow I had to pick up the prescription, book an appointment with the nurse to administer it, and then take the prescription to the pharmacy to pick up the components of the injection. Having cancer was hard work, I was beginning to think I would need a secretary to sort everything out.

I did get all this sorted the next day. In fact I had two or three other prescription items to pick up at the pharmacy anyway. Perhaps I was a bit paranoid but I thought I clocked the pharmacist mentally registering the addition to the normal prescription list. Maybe he was thinking 'ah, prostate cancer to add to his list, what next?'

First injection in January, the last one scheduled for December, nearly three years away – there would be a lot of water under the bridge by the time the hormone therapy was scheduled to finish.

••••

Meanwhile, Neal Johnston was getting his first monthly hormone injection for prostate cancer in his health centre in East Belfast. The hormone was injected into the hip. It stung like hell. And there was a bit of bleeding. Neal had been injected on his right hip. The arrangement was for the left hip to be used the following month. Neal had been doing a bit of internet research on the hormone therapy. There was never any doubt it was going to be the injections, the tablets and the big breasts were not an option. No way. He had discussed the side effects of both the injections and the tablets with his wife Maxine. She was totally supportive – all she wanted was for Neal to still be here in a few years' time, she didn't really mind which option he went for as long as he got through it all.

Neal's two children were equally supportive. Ben was a teacher – science, so he would know something about what was going on and Laura was a GP, who would definitely know what was going on. She was a good sounding board, although he didn't discuss the hormone options with her. That would just be too much. Laura lived in Downpatrick, about 20 miles away. She had been with Neal when the Consultant had broken the news, although she had had to insist that she attended the appointment with her dad, he was a bit more ambivalent about her being there. But Laura knew the significance of '*you may want to bring a friend or relative to accompany you*'.

By the time Neal arrived home the irritation had gone and the injection was like a distant dream. There was just too much living to do to worry about such things.

Prostate cancer was to be confronted like the other life battles. Neal was determined that it was not going to affect him too much. It was to be regarded as a minor inconvenience and kicked into touch as soon as feasibly possible.

••••

When the surgery screen flashed that I should go to Treatment Room 2 for my appointment with Nurse Gibson, I quickly checked that I had the hormone medication in my pocket before heading down the corridor. After confirming why I was here and other formalities, she mixed the active ingredient in the solvent and checked the syringe for air bubbles.

After giving me the injection in my hip, we arranged the next month's appointment. Before leaving, she offered me the patient leaflet with the explanation; 'Jack, you might as well take this leaflet with you. You might want to have a read through it and it will give you an idea of what side effects to expect.'

Of course, I had already been through the side effects with Dr Gavasker and others, but I took the leaflet anyway. Over coffee with Jane we both had a quick look through it. There was little we didn't know, but the almost certain effect on sexual function and the likelihood of having 'hot flushes' were high on the published list. The next few days were certainly going to be interesting but it looked as if some of the side effects were a done deal.

In reality the first side effect to really hit home was the fatigue. A few days after the injection I could barely move. Bedtime came early and afternoon naps became part of the routine. For a couple of hours each afternoon I was absolutely shattered. Not a massive problem as long as I didn't try to do too much. It made sense to put work on the back burner for a while. The way I was feeling I really wasn't going to be too much use anyway.

I was on the ball enough to ring the Urology Department to check if I really needed to attend my appointment there. Things seemed to be happening so fast and it seemed as if I had passed from the care of Urology in the main City Hospital complex to Oncology at the Cancer Centre. Thankfully this was easy enough to sort. Not surprisingly, the receptionist I got through to wouldn't cancel the appointment on her own without checking with the Consultant. But she did ring me the next day to say that he was OK with me cancelling it.

As the weeks wore on the fatigue appeared to be ever present. If it couldn't be cured it had to be managed. Resting, naps and early to bed seemed to be the way forward. But fatigue ceased to be the only side effect. The lack of testosterone in my body was causing my hands to get very dry, dry to the extent they would bleed from a myriad of hacks and open crevices.

Jane had the answer to this. 'Moisturise your hands at every opportunity and also before going to bed at night. Before going to bed, apply loads of lotion and then wear a pair of gloves to stop the lotion rubbing off – in fact I have some specialised pairs ideally suited for this job.'

The fatigue and dry hands seemed to improve slightly in the last week of January, one week before my next injection. It was impossible to say if I was getting used to the hormone therapy or was it a case of the hormone levels having peaked and then dropping as the first monthly cycle was coming to its end.

Getting the second hormone injection sorted was not automatic. I still had to organise the repeat prescription from the GP and get the prescription from the pharmacy. Thankfully the appointment with the nurse had already been done, I had booked this when getting the first injection.

This went on for three months and the side effects slotted into their monthly cycle, peaking after a week and tailing off into the fourth week of the cycle. Around the start of the third cycle I got my appointment letter for the planning scan.

The letter asked me to report to Radiotherapy Reception in the Cancer Centre at 3 pm on Wednesday 12th March for preparation for CT scanning at 4 pm. There was also a leaflet explaining in good detail how the preparation for planning and treatment appointments would work. There were a few good hints. But really nothing that hadn't been explained by the radiotherapist on the last visit except the idea of practising holding half a litre of water in my bladder for an hour or so. In the days before the appointment, once or twice each day I drank 500 ml of water over a short period of time and tried to avoid going to the loo for at least an hour. By the time the planning appointment came round I was able to do it, but only if I avoided drinking anything in the two or three hours beforehand. That understanding was the real benefit in having practised.

By the time the planning appointment came around the daffodils were well up, a flower synonymous with cancer. Yet one of hope. They reminded us that summer was on the way. Jane came with me to this appointment. Although it was a one-off, its format was relatively similar to what the next 37 were going to be like. We arrived early so we went into the coffee shop. Jane had a decaffeinated Americano and I had a German biscuit. I had learnt enough over the previous few days to work out that a coffee at this stage would play havoc; a coffee now and there would be no chance of me taking 500 ml of water and not needing to go to the loo over the next hour.

Still it was hardly a sacrifice. The mood was positive as we were both glad that things were getting underway. At ten minutes to three we headed through the doors into radiotherapy. After handing in the appointment letter we were ushered into a small waiting area running perpendicular to the main corridor running through the department. It seemed fairly busy, there were about ten other people there. I was glad Jane was there on this occasion as most of the men were accompanied.

After a few moments, a young radiotherapist came down to see me. After the introductions, Michelle sat down beside me and started to explain what was going to happen. She was carrying a small box, about the size that would hold a small tube of toothpaste. This contained the micro-enema. Michelle explained that within fifteen minutes of using this I would need to go to the toilet. This would ensure that the bowel was as empty as it could be. This was the first part of the preparation, and in reality the most unpleasant part. After this stage was complete (probably by around 3.25 pm or so, she said), I was to drink 500 ml of water over a relatively short period and not go to the toilet after this. She explained the importance of having a full bladder. While I was not getting any radiation treatment on this occasion, the radiotherapists had to be sure that I could hold the water in the system for up to an hour and, more importantly, the lower abdomen had to be in the same anatomical state for the imaging that was about to take place as it would be when the radiation actually started. Before leaving, Michelle explained that she would come back in about an hour and if there were any problems in the interim (particularly about being able to retain the half litre of water) I should ask the receptionist to call her.

The time dragged. Other patients and their partners seemed better prepared. Some had brought books, *Kindles*, and one had even brought a laptop. The laptop owner seemed to be getting on with his work, being here seemed to be only a minor inconvenience. By the time I returned from the toilet having completed phase one of the planning, Jane was chatting to his wife.

She was full of beans. Her husband had completed 35 of the 37 sessions so he was going to be finished by the end of the week. She had two bits of advice to pass on.

'Bring your own 500 ml bottle of water which would be at ambient temperature by the time it was needed, rather than use the fountains in the Cancer Centre. The cold fountain water will make you run to the loo more quickly.'

That made sense, it seemed good advice. The second piece of advice was a bit more worrying.

'Hopefully, you won't need them, but if I were you I would pack a spare pair of underpants and trousers in your rucksack.'

It was left unsaid, but I assumed this was borne out of experience. I could imagine if you maybe weren't feeling too well or if there were delays, holding on to the 500 ml of water for an hour or more could just be tricky enough on occasions. Something else to worry about.

By the time I had digested the advice, I had taken four small cups of water in quick succession. I had no option but to use the cold water from the fountain as I hadn't brought my own supply. The practice over the previous days and the fact that I hadn't taken a drink in the hours before arriving had paid off. I wasn't under any real pressure by the time Michelle arrived back to collect me.

Jane remained in the waiting room as Michelle and I headed down the corridor to the planning suite. Before entering the suite itself, Michelle asked me to fill in another form and checked that the enema had been used and that I had taken 500 ml of water since I had last been to the loo.

When we entered the planning suite, Enya, another radiotherapist, introduced herself and explained what they were going to do. This done, I removed my shoes and trousers as requested and climbed up on the couch. Michelle and Enya straightened me up and switched the lasers on. There were two moulds, one for my head and one for my ankles to help get me in the correct position. One of the fine green laser beams extended from the roof down to my pelvic area. Two others, one from each side of the room, zoned in on my left and right hips. I was lying on my back and had to keep my head steady so I couldn't see exactly where the lasers were targeting.

Enya was the first to speak, she seemed to be in charge of this part of the operation.

'Jack, just move down the couch a fraction, we want the laser coming from the roof to be positioned exactly above where the prostate lies.'

Once they thought they had it in position, Michelle chipped in, 'Jack do you mind if we shave you a little bit, just so we can mark the position clearly?'

I just nodded. After sorting this out they then turned their attention to the two horizontal beams. A bit more twisting and straightening and I was lined up and locked onto the three laser beams.

The two radiotherapists checked the positioning on their computer monitors. As well as the laser beams defining the correct position the scanner was feeding images back. Once the scanner confirmed I was in the correct position, Michelle used some type of permanent marker to tattoo the positions on my abdomen that were lined up against the laser beams. In reality they were micro-tattoos, and hard to see unless you knew where you were looking.

Enya noted that, 'the images looked good, they have confirmed that the markings are in exactly the correct position and also that your preparation worked well. The bladder and bowel have been prepared as required and they are as far as possible out of the danger zone. Dr Gavasker will review the images but they should be OK. If she is not happy we will need to bring you in again to redo this but I don't think that will happen.'

'Does this often happen, that patients are brought back to go through all this all again?'

'Surprisingly often Jack, we had a couple of patients here this morning who were back for the third time. Thankfully, for both of them it worked out OK today.'

I was just relieved to get through all this without any disasters. For the first time I now felt that the radiation therapy was underway, even if I had to wait for the actual treatment to start.

Michelle reminded me that it would take another six weeks or so to get my personalised program sorted. The images taken today would help the treatment planners and the oncologists work out the best possible regime for me. She added that the program planning would probably be completed and checked by around the end of April. After checking that it was a very early slot in the day that I wanted, Michelle walked me back to Jane in the waiting area. It was nearly 5 pm and things were a lot quieter in the outer foyer. The coffee shop and the newsagents were closed and there were no patients sitting waiting for their radiotherapy slot. Most of the action probably centred on the wards on the upper floors where many patients who were beyond the outpatient stage lay. I really hoped that the radiation would work and that I wouldn't be joining them.

Chapter 14

It seemed that the radiotherapy wouldn't start until around the end of April if up to six weeks was needed to plan the treatment. This was going to take us up into the teeth of Easter. It was hard to imagine that it would start in the days immediately before Easter so we assumed the most likely date was going to be just after the Easter holidays. Nonetheless, the wait was frustrating.

On the way home from the planning scan we discussed what we could do in the intervening time. Jane was keen to organise a week in the sun sometime before Easter. I couldn't agree more. When we got home, we started to scan the internet for ideas.

In the end we got a week in Majorca, the week before the Easter fortnight. The flight times were good and the hotel was well priced for a four star; it would be a different matter for Easter week or in high summer. The hotel had not been open for long this season. It was one of those that closed during the winter.

The holiday came and went. The food was great and the whole experience was very relaxing. Probably a few too many beers, but no big deal. Radiotherapy was barely mentioned. However, the heat made a big difference to my very dry hands, the cracks and hacks all closed over and they were in much better shape by the time we returned. I could understand why some people migrate to hotter climates for health reasons. The fatigue was not an issue either, it wasn't as if we were trying to do too much. But it seems so much easier sitting around doing nothing when you are on holiday and when it is warm.

Before going on holiday I had contacted the Radiotherapy Department to check that it was OK to be away that particular week. It was not an issue and they agreed to ring me a few days after I got back from Majorca. On cue they contacted me on the Thursday before Good Friday. I was to start the Wednesday after Easter week. I was getting fed up with the waiting, life seemed to be on hold.

The Easter weather was good so this prolonged the feel-good factor after returning from Majorca. Over Easter I began practising holding 500 millilitres of water for up to an hour. I had learnt my lesson, it could be done if very little water was taken in the hours before. I also cut down my alcohol content. Feeling thirsty due to dehydration or having too much fluid in the system were both problems in terms of water balance. Real coffee became a no-no. The caffeine irritated the system and also played havoc with keeping the bladder full. Apart from all this I was in reasonable shape as the start date drew near. The fatigue brought on by the hormone therapy was still there but I was becoming better at managing it.

The start date was Wednesday 30 April, two days after I had my fourth hormone injection. Although most of my slots were going to be very early morning, the first session was planned for 10.30 am. Jane wanted to come with me to this appointment but I persuaded her not to. I didn't know how much waiting around there would be. It was the train again. I didn't expect that the radiation would in any way affect my ability to drive, but I wasn't sure how I would feel at the end. I didn't even know if there would be any emotional impact. Impossible to tell in advance, but getting radiotherapy was not something you planned for in the grand scheme of things.

The later start gave me good time to get organised. My rucksack contained spare trousers and a 500 ml bottle of water – I had taken the advice about bringing my own water at ambient temperature. That morning I had toast as usual for breakfast but only one cup of decaffeinated tea. And I had it early. While

I didn't want to be dehydrated when I arrived, I didn't want to have extra water in the system causing problems. It seemed that everything with prostate cancer was a balancing act.

The train got me to the hospital halt in very good time and the short walk from the halt to the Cancer Centre was refreshing. The radiotherapist had explained that my 10.30 appointment was the time I should arrive at on the first day. By the time the preparation was complete it would be at least 11.30 before the actual radiation treatment took place.

Rucksack on back, I entered the Radiotherapy Department, passed the outer reception area and turned into the main treatment block. As I had arranged this first appointment over the phone, I didn't have an appointment letter so I just gave my name to the receptionist in the treatment area. She had been expecting me, she gave me one of the flashing disks and asked me to take a seat. The waiting area was relatively large, being able to hold around fifty people. There were comfortable chairs, nice paintings on the pastel walls and two drinking fountains. The place was very busy, radiotherapists coming and going as were patients. There were about thirty patients and their relatives or friends. Mainly men. Most of the few women who appeared to be patients wore scarves over their heads or hats. It seemed that they had also been on chemotherapy as well as radiotherapy. I wondered how they compared the treatments in terms of side effects. Losing your hair, for a woman, cannot be fun. However, they all seemed to be in great spirits. And they all weren't old. One or two appeared to be in their twenties or thirties. Most people were chatting away, it seemed as if the regulars had formed little social groups. Almost as if they looked forward to the chat. On this first day I didn't really chat to anyone, I was just taking it all in and making sure I did nothing wrong. It also all seemed just a bit unreal. Surreal almost.

Lost in thought, I was brought back to the here and now when my disk started to flash. I looked up at the reception area and could see one of the radiotherapists coming my way. She came and sat down in an empty chair beside me.

'Hello Jack, nice to see you again, I'm Gail, I'm one of the radiotherapists in LA9 – that's the suite you will be having your treatment in. Have you any questions and are you clear about what the preparation involves? It's really just a re-run of what you did when you were in for your planning scan.'

'Yes thanks, Gail.'

'Here is your enema for today. It's now just after 10.30, I'll come back for you at 11.30. If there are any problems ask the receptionist to give me a call. OK, see you soon.'

On her way down to suite LA9, Gail nodded to another patient sitting close to me. He got up and the two of them started chatting as they headed down to LA9. As they clearly knew each other, I assumed that he was someone well into his treatment program. I wondered what he was making of it all.

The enema and its aftermath were unpleasant but straightforward. There is just no way you could find it something to look forward to. That side of the preparation took about 20 minutes. I drank the 500 ml of water within about five minutes, leaving about 35 minutes or so before I was expecting Gail back. After taking the water there was nothing to do other than try to relax. Getting tense wasn't going to help, particularly if I starting thinking I needed to go to the loo.

By the time Gail returned I could have gone to the loo, but wasn't under any real pressure. After checking that the preparation was complete she took me down to LA9. I was 'parked' in the small waiting area just outside the radiation room. I could see that the yellow radiation warning lights outside the suite were on, someone must be in the middle of his/her treatment. In a few minutes, the warning lights went off and two radiotherapists went back into the suite from their computer bay immediately outside. A couple of minutes later, a man who seemed to be in his sixties drifted out and headed back up the corridor and out of the department.

Gail and another radiotherapist brought me into the large room containing the Linear Accelerator, the LA in LA9. I found out later that a linear accelerator is just a particular type of radiation-producing machine that produces high-energy X-rays. The other radiotherapist, Clare, asked me to take my shoes and trousers off but keep underpants and socks on. She then asked me to confirm my date of birth and address. You could only guess at the hassle there would be if someone was given radiation treatment by mistake; front page fodder if anything was. I could see my name and details of the radiation program I was having on a monitor well up the wall. The couch, platform or bed, I wasn't sure what to call it, was lowered to a level that made it easy to climb onto. It had also been moved out away from directly under the accelerator. No doubt to stop a patient banging his or her head on it, not great for the head and certainly not great for the expensive equipment. Gail had placed a couple of body moulds on the couch. One was for my head and the other was for my ankles. These seemed to be to keep me steady and in the position they wanted.

'Jack, climb up onto the couch and lie on your back. Put your head in the mould at the top and the bottom of your legs in the other mould. We will adjust their positions if necessary.'

I climbed onto the couch and lay down as Clare had asked. As I was getting comfortable, the green laser lights were switched on. My head was raised just enough so that I could see the green laser hitting somewhere on my lower abdomen. Clare and Gail were on either side of the couch checking the positions of the horizontal laser beams coming from each side of the room.

Gail added, 'we are just going to add temporary markings with these pens to the permanent markings you got at the planning scan. It will help us make sure you are in the correct position as the permanent markings are so small and difficult to see. The lasers have to hit the tiny tattoos you were given. Just slide your underpants down a little, we need to line the laser from the roof up with the permanent mark just above the prostate.'

As I did this, Clare carefully placed a large sheet of paper towel over me just below where the prostate marking was.

'Just fractionally down the couch a bit, Jack. Yes that's great.' At that stage Gail took hold of my hips and straightened me a fraction. The two radiotherapists confirmed to each other that I was in the right position. They were discussing numbers or angles that made little sense to me.

'We are going to take some images before the radiation is switched on. This is to check that the preparation is good and that that everything is lined up correctly. It will make a bit of a buzzing sound and the machine will move around you taking images from different angles. When that's complete the radiation lights will come on – you will hear the clunk. Then the radiation will start. It will make a different buzzing sound and will only last for a few minutes. We will be watching you from outside, if there is a problem raise your arm. OK, see you in a few minutes.'

With that, Clare and Gail left the room and disappeared into their computer bay outside.

I kept very still as the whirring and buzzing started. I knew this was just the imaging as out of the corner of my eye I could see that the radiation warning signs were not lit up. After a short time, probably only a few minutes, I could both hear and see the radiation warnings come on. This was it. There seemed to be a short pulse of radiation, then it would stop as the machine adjusted position to zap me from another angle. Then it would start again. Of course I could feel nothing. In fact remaining in the one position for a short period of time was actually very relaxing. Therapeutic almost. After a few minutes, the rotating arms of the accelerator stopped and there was no more noise bar the radiation warning going off. Then Clare and Gail came back in and helped me down from the couch. They kept me waiting until the couch was lowered much closer to ground level. After getting dressed, I threw my rucksack over my shoulder and walked out into the corridor space that stretched between the two rows of radiotherapy suites.

At that point, Oonagh, the leader of LA9, gave me an appointment sheet with all my session times printed on it. The list of appointments stretched down almost all the length of the A4 page – not surprising as there were 36 more sessions. She also gave me two boxes of enemas, a total of 36. Thankfully these were able to fit into my rucksack. Oonagh also pointed out that as my appointment times were 8.30 am from now on, I would need to be here by 7.30 and that preparation would probably need to begin before any of the radiotherapists were in. In other words there would be nobody here to keep me right. Hopefully I could manage on my own.

I could think about all this later, my immediate priority was to get to a loo. My irritated bladder had had enough. What state would it be in by the time we got to number 37?

Chapter 15

I arrived home around 3pm and felt absolutely shattered. Jane made a pot of tea and we sat down to discuss the morning's events. Not having any children meant there was no one else to bounce things off.

After a cup of tea and a scone, I lay down on the sofa and watched the cricket on *Sky* for a couple of hours. It was probably not only the stress of the first radiotherapy session, it was also only a few days since I had the hormone injection and I tended to feel worse in the week or so after getting it.

I remained tired throughout the day and ended up heading off to bed around nine. Before doing this I checked my rucksack. I took most of the enemas out and stored them in my wardrobe, well out of sight. That only left two or three in the bag, enough to carry at any one time. The raincoat, spare trousers and a packet of tissues were neatly packed and I threw a book in just in case. There was a fair bit of waiting around and the possibility of the machines breaking down was always there, or even the rota being disrupted due to someone needing to be slotted in in a hurry. But before falling asleep I made up my mind that I would drive tomorrow. Starting on a Wednesday was an easy lead in. It meant only three days before getting a break. And to make thing even better, there was no radiotherapy the following Monday, May Day.

I had a good night's sleep. But it was an early start on Thursday as it was going to be most days. I was up at 5.45 and had a quick shower before bringing Jane a mug of tea. I made myself a small cup, a round of toast, and climbed back into bed to watch the start of BBC *Breakfast* while having my tea; if I was only going to have one cup I was going to enjoy it. I had organised my clothes the night before so getting dressed took no time and I was ready to hit the road by 6.30. As I left the village I did a mental check ensuring that I had everything I needed. I had just remembered the bottle of water and no more, but was content that nothing critical had been left behind. It was bright but the roads were quiet. Had it not been for the prospect of going through the whole enema experience I could almost have been looking forward to the trip. My appointment was for 8.30 so the planning had to be underway by 7.30. I hoped to be in the hospital by 7 or so to avoid any rushing. I wanted everything to be nice and calm. Getting to the hospital was very straightforward. The M1 Sprucefield 'car park' wasn't an issue at 6.45; it no doubt would materialise later to the frustration of so many drivers. Even parking at the hospital was no problem. I was able to park on the Ground Floor of the multi-storey. By the time I entered the revolving doors of the Cancer Centre it was just turning 7. Not that there was much action at that time. The newsagent and coffee shop were both closed and there was only one other man in the foyer as far as I could see. He was sitting in the central chair in one of the semi-circular rows. I could only assume that he was here for the same thing. I had a few seconds to make up by mind whether to ignore him, say a quick hello and sit somewhere else, or actually sit close to him and perhaps pass the time by chatting.

In the end I sat beside him.

'Hi, I'm Jack Steenson. Do you mind if I sit beside you?'

'Of course not, please sit down, I'm Neal Johnston and I suspect we might both be here for the same reason. Are you here for radiotherapy, Jack?'

'Yes, I've prostate cancer and this is my second of thirty seven sessions.'

'Snap, it is also my second of thirty seven sessions. Join the 37 club. What time is your appointment, Jack?'

'I'm on at 8.30 in LA9, what about you?'

'I'm on at 8.40, also in LA9, I must be immediately after you. The doors through to radiotherapy are not open until 7.30, so we have to start our preparation here. The joys!'

'I don't mind the loading with water, but I absolutely hate the enema,' I replied.

'I would be surprised if anyone enjoyed that,' retorted Neal with a grin on his face.

We both chatted away as we knew we had a few minutes before we needed to get underway. Staff began to filter in. Two young women dressed in black uniform were going to the coffee dock, another one to the newsagents, a nurse going upstairs and another couple who sat down immediately opposite us on the other semi-circular row of chairs. They also took the central chairs; as far away from us as they possibly could be – a psychologist would have had a field day in here. We could only assume that one was a patient and the other one an accompanying spouse or partner. There was good people watching here just as there was everywhere else.

Just as the radiotherapy doors were automatically but audibly unlocked at 7.30, I lifted an enema box out of my rucksack.

'Neal, I better go and get this started. I'm going to use one of the loos in the foyer. They have the yellow medical disposal bins so I assume it's OK for us to start this out here.'

As I headed off, Neal quipped, 'absolutely, I'm sure ordinary visitors have no idea of what goes on in these loos.'

I wasn't sure what an ordinary visitor was. There would not be too many people in here that weren't fairly closely associated with cancer.

I was back in my seat in five minutes and at that stage Neal got up to start his ordeal. When he came back we decided to head into the radiotherapy waiting area. At 7.30 the receptionist was not yet on duty so we left our appointment lists on her desk and sat down. One or two radiotherapists were already in, checking rotas and I assume other administrative tasks.

We sat down together at the edge of the waiting room in a position where we could see most of what was going on. We had barely got chatting again and it was time for me to return to the loo. That morning for the first time I realised that there were times when it was very hard to be sure when the enema had actually stopped working. I was a bit worried that I could start the water loading and then have to run to the loo again. That would be a bit of a shambles, but I'm sure it happens often enough. Let's just hope it doesn't happen to me, not yet anyway.

The time had drifted round to 7.50 and I was pretty sure I didn't need to revisit the loo. I was starting to panic that I was leaving it very tight for the water loading. So I drank my bottle of water over five or six minutes just in case. It was easy enough to drink it but time would tell how much pressure it was going to put me under. And I wasn't really sure if drinking 500 ml very quickly would put me under a bit more pressure than drinking it just a bit more slowly. Learning from experience was going to play a big part in getting through all this.

As the time approached 8.30 we could see more patients and more radiotherapists arriving. The receptionist also arrived and the first thing she appeared to do was to bring the appointment cards already sitting on her desk to the appropriate LA suites. Most of the radiotherapists seemed to head to their respective stations via one of the water fountains to fill their personal water bottles. I could appreciate that it would be much nicer drinking the cold water than carrying water from home. But of course they didn't have to hold on to it for forty minutes. Perhaps, the suites were warmer or had less humidity than I thought, or perhaps they were just good at keeping themselves hydrated. Keeping hydrated seems to be a young person's thing, certainly a young woman thing.

Just after 8.30 Clare came up from LA9 to the waiting area. She spotted Neal and myself – not bad recognising us after only one day, but I suppose it was helped by the waiting area being relatively empty at this time of the morning. She gave us back our appointment cards and asked us to follow her down to the small waiting area dedicated to LA9. This was immediately outside the radiation room itself but was ideally situated for patients to observe the radiotherapists in their computer bays. The radiation light was on as we arrived and two radiotherapists seemed to be using computer monitors to follow what was taking place inside. After we were sitting for a few minutes, Clare came back and told us there was going to be a slight delay.

'One of the other machines has a small fault and we have taken one of the patients scheduled for that one. We are going to squeeze him in next, so that will delay you two for about ten minutes. Can you cope OK?'

'We will be fine', replied Neal.

'And what about you Jack?'

'Hopefully, I'll be fine too, as long as the wait isn't too long.'

We watched the new patient enter the radiation room and then the routine that followed. A few minutes later the radiotherapists came out, wiped their hands with gel and climbed onto their chairs in front of their monitors. The radiation lights came on. But ten minutes became fifteen minutes; maybe this patient was not a prostate patient and his treatment was a bit more complex and longer? Anyway, Clare, who was not involved with him came over to see how we were doing.

'Are you lasting OK, gents?'

Neal nodded but I was getting under pressure.

'Clare, I'm getting under a bit of pressure, will the wait be much longer?'

'Hopefully just another couple of minutes, but if you are really bursting we'll try to fit you in somewhere else.'

'If it is only a couple of minutes I'll last, but not if it is much longer.'

'OK.'

I'm sure this was a conversation Clare and the others had many times over the course of a week. And there probably were some accidents too; people just trying to wait longer than their bladder could cope. And of course I was on medication for an overactive and irritable bladder anyway, so mine didn't seem to be in great shape to start with. I was just merging from the pressure to pain stage when Clare came and asked me to come into the radiation room. As I walked down the short corridor the previous patient came out. On the way in Clare checked my name and address and date of birth. Probably to speed things up. It certainly suited me but also suited the team; I'm sure they wanted to get back on schedule as quickly as possible.

I didn't waste much time in taking my shoes and trousers off. Gail and another radiotherapist came into the room. Gail introduced her as Eithne, a student on placement. I climbed onto the couch and Eithne and Clare helped get me in position and in the right shape to slot into the head and leg moulds.

'Move down just a fraction and bend your knees just a bit more,' said Clare as Gail switched on the lasers. Clare and Eithne were positioned, one on each side of the couch and they used non-permanent markers to make my tattoos a bit more obvious. Then it was a matter of lining my markings exactly with the laser beams. Once this was done the girls left the room switching on the radiation program as they departed. There was nothing to do except lie as still as possible as the machine moved, firing its pulses of radiation from a range of different angles as it did so. After a few minutes the now-familiar clunk of the radiation being switched off and today's program being complete could be heard, immediately preceding Gail and Eithne returning to the room. I had already worked out that the radiotherapists shared the different tasks. The one sorting you out at the end was often not the one in charge of lining you up at the start.

It was Gail who spoke first. 'Jack don't move until we lower the couch, you are quite a height up there.' As the couch was lowered she chatted away, 'you might find that the skin around the micro-tattoos gets a bit sore after a period of time. This is just the effect of the lasers hitting the same position of skin each day. It is probably best if you don't try to remove the marks we put on each day to help us line you up. We put these on to avoid mistaking one of the tattoos for a mole or a freckle or something similar. Our markings will rub off fairly quickly anyway.'

This was a minor problem at this stage; it was well over an hour since I had taken the 500 ml of water and it was a miracle I was holding on. I got dressed in record time, thanked Gail and Eithne and we said our goodbyes as I headed down the corridor to very welcome relief in the first loo I could find. I had enough time to wish Neal all the best as I passed him in the corridor. He still had another ten minutes or so to go before he could leave but he didn't appear to be under too much pressure, lucky him.

I replayed the morning in my mind as I drove home. It was hard to imagine that I could have done anything else differently. At least that was day two complete, only thirty five more to go! I was under enough pressure today, what will it be like once the radiotherapy side effects kick in? I wasn't really fit for too much for the rest of the day but did manage to go with Jane and do a bit of light shopping in the afternoon. Yet again, bed came early and was most welcome.

Getting up for day three was almost routine. The last day of the week before a three day break reminded me what a Friday was like in full-time work. It was a beautiful morning and the sun was rising over the horizon. The walk from the high-rise car park was pleasant and people were scurrying about as the busy hospital was gearing up for the day. As I reached the door of the Cancer Centre a couple of smokers were coming out for what was probably their first smoke of the morning, fairly incongruous I thought. Neal arrived at the same time, coming from the direction of the main university complex.

We sat in the same seats as we did on Thursday, creatures of habit.

'Hi Neal, another good day.'

'Yes, this would all be much harder if we were trying to do this in the howling wind and bucketing rain in December. You would have a day's work over you before you even got here.'

There was a bit more chat about the weather and other fairly trivial things and then we got down to business. It was starting to work like clockwork, we barely had to check the time before we knew what we had to do. Once the doors to radiotherapy were open we were both in a position to be able to walk through and down to reception. Again the same seats. It seemed to be like a school staffroom, everyone appeared to migrate to 'their' seat. We left our appointment cards on the receptionist's table. As we both dropped ours together, I noticed that Neal had carefully drawn a line through the last two days; he was clearly ticking them off as the sessions came and went.

Nipping to the loo, drinking water, patients and staff arriving, nothing was static for too long. We were chatting away when a middle-aged couple came in and sat down directly opposite us. We assumed that the lady was the patient as she was wearing a scarf around her head. While it looked OK, it was not exactly fashionable so we guessed it was to hide the hair loss. Perhaps she had been on chemotherapy before coming for radiotherapy. There was a further clue when she started loading with water. It must be cancer in the lower abdomen or pelvic area, I thought. Perhaps ovarian?

'Hi, I'm Mandy, she said after we had been sitting for a few minutes. This is my first day in radiotherapy today and this is my husband Iain.'

'Hi, I'm Jack and this is Neal, we have really only started too. This is our third day, just the thirty four more to go for us!'

'That's a lot,' Mandy replied, 'I have twenty sessions here but this is following on the heels of chemo.'

'That must be tough' – it was Neal's turn to chip in. And that was how it started. Every morning we would sit and chat about trivial things, personal things, medical things, whatever we fancied. Iain was good craic too. He was a civil servant; a statistician of all things, working on census and other mind-numbing data. Perhaps a little unkindly, I thought he looked like a civil servant. We had plenty of jokes about civil servants but at least Iain did go into work after Mandy's daily treatment was finished and he had taken her home. Neal and I weren't too unhappy we had finished with the rigours of full-time work. I wasn't sure that I'd be too keen to head into work after being through all this each morning.

Mandy's appointment was for LA6 at 8.30. Just as she was collected by one of her team of radiotherapists, Eithne came down to collect Neal and me. Neal had another ten minutes to wait in the LA9 waiting area but neither of us seemed to be under too much pressure this particular morning.

We were old hands now we thought; we knew what to expect in the radiation room. Gail and Clare were again on duty in LA9 and they were also looking forward to the long weekend break. Gail was going up north to visit her mum and Clare and her boyfriend were going walking in the Mourne Mountains.

As Neal and I crossed in the short corridor leading to the radiation room, we wished each other a good weekend. As I walked through the corridor leading out of radiotherapy, I couldn't help smiling to myself. Yes, the first week was complete and I didn't even need to rush to the loo. Happy days.

Chapter 16

Much as I enjoyed the long weekend, in a strange sort of way I was glad when Tuesday morning came round. Perhaps I was just keen to get the counter ticking again and notch up the next four of the thirty seven radiotherapy sessions during the week.

Neal arrived in the Cancer Centre just a few minutes after I did. We sat down in our usual seats and started chatting about the weekend. Neal clearly had a good time as he couldn't wait to get started.

'Jack, we have had a very busy weekend. As I told you last week, I am not letting this treatment get on top of me. Life is going to be as normal as I can make it. We went down to see Laura in Downpatrick at the weekend. We took her Canadian canoe to Sheepland harbour and spent a couple of hours paddling up and down the coast.'

'Glad you had the energy Neal, you don't suffer fatigue the way I do.'

'Yes, it is strange the way those hormone injections affect the two of us in different ways. They don't seem to affect me at all and yet they nearly flatten you.'

'Too right Neal, we just have different metabolisms; maybe it will be the other way round when the radiotherapy side effects kick in, but hopefully that will not be for a while yet. We have enough to keep us going for the time being.'

We had got to the stage where we didn't need to think too much about the routine. As in the previous week, we started the preparation in the outer foyer at the Cancer Centre entrance and at seven thirty moved through to the main radiotherapy waiting area. Neal was still striking off each day very neatly on his appointment sheet whereas mine was getting a bit dog-eared.

I was just finishing my water loading when Mandy and Iain came and sat down opposite us. The four of us were in the same seats as we had been when we last met.

'Hi gents,' started Mandy, 'hope you had a good weekend.'

We uttered a joint 'yes and what about you.' I think Neal was champing at the bit to continue the story about the canoe trip before Iain got in first.

'Mandy had a bit of a rough time, she was sick much of Saturday and Sunday. Thankfully she was much better yesterday.'

'Was it linked to the treatment?' I asked.

I wasn't sure if Mandy really wanted Iain to bring her not being well into the public domain, but she responded with, 'difficult to say, I haven't really been that great over the past few weeks.'

There wasn't really much more that could be said without it getting very personal, so we did get around to hearing about Neal's canoe trip. It sounded great fun. His daughter Laura had prepared a picnic and they had pulled into a little rocky cove and had had a lovely time relaxing in the sun on the shore.

Neal went on, 'Laura kept telling me to take it easy, but I was fine. It was far too nice a day to be sitting around, so I was keen to be back on the water again, paddling about. She did warn me that I mightn't be quite so chirpy when I'm into the radiotherapy a few more weeks. All the more reason for getting out and about now.'

We couldn't argue with that.

At eight thirty it was Toni who came up to collect Neal and myself. She hadn't met us before so she had to read out our names. However, I think Gail had told her where we were likely to be sitting so she was hovering in our direction anyway. Toni was tall with straight, shiny black hair. She was also chatty so the three of us were in conversation before we had reached LA9.

As normal, Neal was parked in the LA9 waiting area while I was taken through. Everything seemed to be on time.

Gail was already in the radiation room setting up the moulds on the couch. 'No Clare today,' I asked.

'No, she's in LA10, just across the way; one of their regulars took an extra day's holiday to make it a *really* long weekend.'

'Nice for her, but did you have a nice weekend, Gail?'

'Yes thanks Jack, it was great, I was up visiting my mum on the North Coast and I brought my boyfriend, Steve, home for the first time.'

'And how did that go down? It can be an interesting experience doing that.'

'Really well, mum loved him.'

'That's great Gail, an important hurdle to get over.' She laughed at that.

Then it was time to get down to business. Toni checked my date of birth and address as Gail lowered the couch. I got undressed and positioned myself as best I could once I got prostrate and organised within the moulds. It didn't take them long to get me lined up with the lasers and the next thing I heard was 'see you in a few minutes Jack' as the two of them disappeared out into the corridor. Then the whirring and buzzing started as fraction four was underway.

Less than ten minutes later I was on my way out of radiotherapy, job done. The excellent weather was clearly continuing into midweek. Rather than rush home I decided to call into the coffee dock for a coffee and something to eat. I ordered a decaffeinated Americano and a bacon roll. I got installed beside a small round table at the corner and decided to watch the world go by for the next half hour. And it did. The place was frantic and it wasn't quite nine yet, perhaps that's why. It would probably quieten down soon after nine as the staff returned to their stations.

Although a small room, that morning there were ambulance staff, dietitians, nurses, doctors dressed in their scrubs and a number of patients and their partners present. The noisy group of casually dressed young people at one table were probably students on medical placement of one form or another.

As I was just finishing the bacon roll – nice but a bit greasy, bearing in mind how my stomach was feeling - Neal popped his head around the door. 'Hi Jack, I saw you sitting at the window as I was heading out, do you fancy the two of us having a coffee on Friday, to sign off week two so to speak?'

'Excellent idea.'

'Great, see you tomorrow.'

I enjoyed the buzz and the people watching. I texted Jane to explain I would be a bit later home. At around nine thirty I headed up to the car park, checking that I had my car park voucher in my wallet. Regular radiotherapy patients had the benefit of free parking which was certainly a bonus.

Wednesday passed without incident. Although, just as I was getting down from the couch Gail mentioned that I would be seeing the review radiographer after my session on Thursday. 'It's just routine Jack, there is always a meeting in the second week. Everything is going well, isn't it? You don't have any side effects from the radiotherapy, not yet anyway?'

'No, all well so far on that front.' I could see the significance in Gail's 'not yet.'

After the Thursday session Clare, who was back in LA9, walked me up to the waiting room for the review radiotherapist. I didn't have to wait too long. After being taken into the small consulting room the review radiotherapist introduced herself. 'Hello Jack, I'm Anna, I'm a review radiographer. One of my roles is to check to see how you are getting on with the radiotherapy. Have you any questions, first of all?'

'Not a lot, things seem to be going OK, but when will the radiotherapy side effects start? The side effects I have from the hormone therapy are bad enough.'

'Jack, I wouldn't worry about the side effects yet. You may or may not get any side effects at all and the actual side effects you may get will not necessarily be the same as everyone else. There is no set pattern, everyone is different.'

'I appreciate that, but there is a good chance I will get side effects, isn't there?'

'Yes there is. And as I've said, the side effects and the severity of the side effects differ from person to person. Also, some people start getting them around half way through their radiotherapy treatment and others don't start getting them until the treatment is nearly finished, but you are unlikely to be getting any for another two or three weeks at least. Are you worried about the diarrhoea?'

'Yes, I'm starting to get it. Nothing too bad, but certainly different to before the radiotherapy started.'

'Jack, that is almost certainly due to the effects of the enemas at this stage. You have been on them for over a week now. They are going to make a difference to your system, it will not be the radiotherapy yet.'

After that we discussed the treatment in general for a few minutes and then Anna came back to hormone therapy side effects. I mentioned the fatigue as being the worst. Anna said that she would get me some leaflets on fatigue and leave them with Clare or Gail, who would pass them on to me.

Even with the appointment with Anna, I was leaving the Cancer Centre just after nine. It was great the way things seemed so organised, no unnecessary waiting around.

Coming back to the centre on Friday morning reminded me what it was like when I was in full time work. The traffic into the city was always lighter on a Friday. There was also the feeling that the weekend was coming. I had largely lost this when in part-time work. It took the routine of the radiotherapy to bring it back.

Even though I was early, Neal was already in his seat by the time I arrived. Over the last couple of days, another prostate patient had joined us in the outer seats. Sean usually came in about twenty past seven; his appointment wasn't until nine but his wife dropped him off on her way to work. He didn't mind the waiting. It was warm and there was plenty to see.

Everything went as normal in terms of the radiotherapy that day. Gail, Clare and Eithne were in LA9. They were also looking forward to their weekends. They chatted away about what they were going to do and it was nice the way they included me in the loop, asking what I was up to. The friendliness and community spirit that developed as radiotherapy progressed was comforting, there was no doubt about that.

As Neal and I did our usual crossover as I was leaving the radiation room and he was entering, I mentioned that I would wait for him in the semi-circular row in the outer foyer. I didn't particularly want to go in to the coffee dock and hog a table waiting for Neal to arrive if it was busy. He was only about another ten minutes, obviously his treatment had gone to plan too. Neal sat down in the corner as I ordered the decaffeinated coffees and scones. There was a bit of a queue, but it was moving quickly. It was nice to get into the seat and have a bit of down time. We hadn't done a full five day week yet, with the Bank Holiday this week and only starting on the Wednesday in the previous week, but I was tired. The routine was almost like work.

Once we started our coffee, we started to chat. We immediately started doing what the leaflets tell us not to do, we compared side effects. 'Jack, things are going well but I really hate those enemas.

You never know when their effect is finished. Sometimes even after I get home, I'm having to rush to the loo.'

'I know, it is not an exact science, sometimes I'm not too sure either. Although, I am coping a bit better with the water loading, than I was. The fatigue is still my biggest hassle and look at you, no fatigue at all!' We compared notes over only drinking decaffeinated coffee, no alcohol during the week and only a very light breakfast with one cup of decaffeinated tea before coming in. We both were making sure we did as little as possible to complicate the water loading or further irritate our lower guts, which were clearly coming under a fair degree of pressure.

We chatted a bit about the football; being early May, the Premier League was coming to its climax. We contemplated a second coffee, briefly, but both agreed this could put unnecessary pressure on our already pressurised bladders. And then it was time to go. As we went our separate ways, I realised that the next time we would see each other we would be in week three. Things were moving on.

Chapter 17

Monday 12 May was the start of week three and the start of the first five day week Neal and I were facing. The excellent weather was still with us, the nights were still shortening and neither of us had developed any side effects linked to the radiotherapy. Although I was still often tired as a result of the hormone therapy, the radiotherapy itself didn't seem to be causing too much of a strain just yet. The internet and some patients much further down the process warned us that this was very likely to change.

Jane had said that she would like to come along on the Monday. She only mentioned this on Sunday evening. I was pleased on many fronts. The company would be nice on the way in. It would be nice for her to see Neal, Mandy, Iain and Sean; she was starting to hear so much about them that she would be able to put faces to names. We headed off at 6.30 as normal and arrived just before 7, also as normal. Unbeknown in advance to us, Neal also had company. Doctor daughter Laura was with him. As soon as the introductions were complete, the chat was bouncing back and forth between the ladies as Neal and I were getting on with things. They appeared not to take us under their notice. Sean arrived just before the doors opened at seven thirty. Laura and Jane headed into the coffee shop as it opened while the three men drifted into radiotherapy. By the time the girls joined us in the radiotherapy waiting area, Iain and Mandy were also there and the time was rattling along.

Toni arrived at 8.30 on the dot and swept Neal and myself away from the social chit chat. As usual it was LA9 we were destined for. Gail was also there as was Eithne. There was something different about Eithne. I couldn't work it out at first but when Gail started bantering her about who she was taking to the university ball later in the week, I realised it was false tan. She looked well and a closer look indicated that she had had her hair done as well. Gail regaled us about her university leavers' ball; it was clear it wasn't really all that long ago. The smile on her face suggested it brought back nice memories. At the end of the session Eithne said that Tuesday would be her last day on placement and she wished me well just in case she didn't see me then. It was a busy and important few weeks for Eithne too. After the big evening out, the series of interviews for upcoming radiotherapy posts would take place.

The rest of the week was reasonably straightforward. Clare was back in LA9 by the Friday after being in one of the other suites. It seemed that many of the radiographers preferred to be settled in one place, working with the same colleagues in the main and also with the same patients. Others weren't so fussed, they didn't mind drifting from one suite to another on different days.

Friday became quiz day. Gail asked me to describe the colour of Clare's hair as we were getting set up for the radiotherapy. Clare had had it done on the Thursday evening in anticipation of a big event she and her boyfriend were going to on Saturday. Gail could barely stop laughing as she asked, 'Jack, exactly what colour do you think Clare's hair is today? You get a prize if you get it correct.'

'Lilac.'

'Sorry, out of luck,' and then more laughs. 'We'll tell you the answer on Monday, by then hopefully someone will have got it right.'

Friday was also coffee day. Neal and I decided for a change we would not have it in the Cancer Centre coffee dock. We were going to break out and go offsite so to speak. We had it in the Queens' University Students Union. A decaffeinated Americano each and slightly warmed raspberry and white chocolate scone seemed a nice way to finish the week. Although it was only ten in the morning when we headed for our cars, for us the weekend had started.

••••

Week four would take us almost to the halfway point. It would have taken us beyond half way if the first two weeks hadn't been truncated. It also gave us the answer to the great quiz; apparently the colour was 'plum with a hint of lilac' or so it had said on the box I was informed. More to the point, Clare and her boyfriend Alex had a great day on Saturday, they had been at her cousin's wedding.

Neal was also in chirpy mood. On Tuesday morning we were sitting just before half eight waiting for us to get the call to LA9 when Gail, body warmer on, walked down the corridor into the waiting area. Neal caught her eye and with a grin on his face starting tapping his watch. Gail spotted him and retorted with a mischievous 'still three minutes to go, I'll be up for the pair of you on time.' And so she was, at eight thirty on the button.

For some reason that morning I was finding it hard to hold on to the water. I badly needed to pee. There was no particular reason; I had no more to drink that morning than normal and everything was running on time. It became most obvious when I was lying on the couch but there was nothing I could do at that stage but see it through. When the whirring started I knew immediately what the different tone was. They were imaging before doing the radiation. This of course meant that it was all going to take that little bit longer. I did last, but not without a bit of squirming about; sharp stabbing pain alternating with feeling nothing at all. Gail had told me in one of my first sessions that the imaging takes place every five days. They do it for a number of reasons including checking that the preparation is still working well. But also to check that patients remain in place when getting the radiation. Not much point in being lined up accurately to the lasers by the radiotherapists if you then shift slightly out of position when the radiation gets going.

The shock came the following morning, the Wednesday. They were imaging me again. When Clare came in to get me down from the couch, I checked this out.

'Yes, Jack we are going to be imaging you for the next few days.'

'Assume I've done something wrong.' I was dreading hearing that some part of the preparation had started to go wrong.

'You were just a bit out of tolerance in your positioning on Tuesday, we have a margin of 3 mm. It's not much so if you move at all after we have you in position the monitors will pick it up. There wasn't much in it but enough to make the difference.'

So the imaging was to continue for the rest of the week and into the following week to make sure I was remaining in position. Not uncommon I was told. By the time Neal and I were chatting over our coffee on Friday he was able to tell me that he was on extended imaging as well. Still, week four was done, by this time next week we would be well over half way.

Chapter 18

It was during week five that things started going askew. Almost imperceptibly at first, things started getting that little bit more out of kilter. It all started well enough. Everything ran to time and the staff continued to be both professional and friendly.

Although as pleasant as ever, Gail had started to ask how I was keeping and did I have any side effects due to the radiotherapy. She already knew about the hormone side effects and had ensured that I was given as much information as possible to help cope with the fatigue. Maybe she did this with everyone or perhaps I was doing something that triggered it. Maybe it was the fact that I needed the extra imaging due to not being able to lie still on the couch for a few minutes. Anyhow, it was the greater urgency to pee that I first noticed. In fact it was Jane who really noticed it first. Maybe I was having to get out of bed quicker or nipping to the loo during the night started to resemble a squaddie's forced-march rather than the nocturnal amble it should be.

The onset was quick and the severity extreme when this particular side effect arose. Again it became a management thing. I only had half a cup of tea in the morning before heading out and nothing to drink after teatime in the evening. Apart from the Friday treat, I had to abandon the occasional cup of decaffeinated coffee after treatment. Although I invariably visited the loo immediately after my session in LA9 and also went home straight after coming out of the coffee dock, the pressure would build up long before I got home. This was OK if I was on the train, but a nightmare if in the car. It wasn't hard to work out why this particular side effect had kicked in. The already-damaged bladder, courtesy of the benign enlargement of the prostate over many years, was being further aggravated by high-energy X-ray radiation. True, the water loading each morning was helping push it out of the way of the radiation beam, but some damage was a given.

Not to be outdone, the intestines were also getting a hammering. And they were starting to let me know. Big time. Again, the daily enema was a protective measure keeping the delicate tissue out of harm's way as far as possible, but collateral radiation damage cannot be avoided it seems. The internet in its many prostate cancer sites highlights increased urgency to pee and diarrhoea as common side effects of radiation treatment for prostate cancer. Although I didn't see it mentioned anywhere, the radiation combined with the effect of enemas creating unnatural conditions in the lower gut probably make things even worse.

Anyway, it all added more hassle and stress. The daily preparation before the radiation treatment became a lot more unpredictable. Trips into town or home had to be planned around the availability of loos and life became less spontaneous. Eating little, but often, became the norm.

The Thursday of week five was Mandy's last session of radiotherapy. Iain was there too. She brought Neal, Sean and myself a cup-cake each, each nicely wrapped in lime green tissue paper and each in a little cardboard bag with string handles. Mandy and Iain had been good company. They were Cancer Centre veterans compared to Neal and I; she had been through chemotherapy upstairs before coming down to the Radiotherapy Department. The chat was good each morning and covered everything under the sun, everything that is except our medical conditions. There were no more comments from Iain about Mandy being sick at home after that initial disclosure. Mandy had probably put paid to that. Even on this last day in radiotherapy she was not looking well. Pasty with no colour and dull, sad eyes. Drawn.

As Neal and I were taken down to LA9, Mandy and Iain were still in their seats. By the time we came out from our sessions they would probably be gone we knew, Mandy getting her final fraction of radiation and Iain in the coffee bar or out for a short walk as he tended to do.

On Mandy's last day I had an appointment with the Consultant immediately after my own session. Gail walked me round to the small waiting room. A couple of days earlier I had my bloods taken so that a PSA value would be available for this meeting. And it was.

'Hello Jack, I'm Heather Maxwell, one of the Consultants, nice to meet you.' She was young and pretty and her informal approach was probably a reflection of her age. 'You are over halfway through your radiotherapy, how are you getting on?'

'Not too bad, but the side effects are really starting to kick in. I've had the hormone therapy side effects for some time now, the hot flushes, the very dry skin and the fatigue and I'm now starting to get some radiotherapy ones as well. But I suppose this is to be expected.'

'The problem is Jack, that everyone is different. It is impossible to predict with different people. So which ones do you think are down to the radiotherapy?'

'Diarrhoea and not getting much warning when I need to pee. They have both got a lot worse over the last week.'

'That's not surprising Jack, they are very common at this stage of the radiotherapy. With locally advanced prostate cancer the radiotherapy is targeting the whole pelvic zone. In reality the organs there are getting a bit of a battering. The one piece of good news I can give you is that most of the side effects will settle down, probably within weeks, after your have stopped the radiotherapy. However, it is very possible they could get worse before they get better. It would be unusual for them to be at their peak at this stage of your treatment.'

We chatted a bit about the various options. Different drugs that could be taken to reduce the effects of the diarrhoea, cream to use on my hands and so on, but in reality she admitted that it was really a case of managing things as best I could. The PSA was 0.07, miniscule compared to previous readings but hardly a surprising value. If my bladder and gut were getting hammered by the radiotherapy, the prostate itself was getting obliterated.

And really that was how things drifted on through the last few weeks of radiotherapy. The side effects did get slightly worse and there were other appointments with the review radiographers just to check how things were going.

My final day was Monday 23 June. It was also Neal's final day too. We decided to turn the clock back and go out for a couple of pints when we were finished. It was like finishing 'A' levels, finishing university, getting results; things like that *had* to be celebrated in the bar. For weeks we had been counting down and the big day finally arrived. Neal's appointment card was still in pristine condition, but mine was covered in coffee stains with the edges torn off.

Sean still had a couple of weeks to go but he had become friendly with a number of other patients whose appointments were scheduled at his time, just a bit later than the two of us. It was Gail that came up to collect us and take us down to LA9 for the final time. Although we had been doing this from the start, two patients being taken down to a suite at the same time seemed a bit unusual; most patients were collected and taken down to their suites individually. Perhaps it was because Neal and I were always sitting together and clearly got on well. It was easier for the staff, one getting zapped and one in the breech so to speak.

Gail was her usual bubbly self, joking away and asking us how we were going to cope when we weren't coming to the Cancer Centre each day. Neal reassured her that we would cope. As Neal was parked in the LA9 waiting bay I was taken through into the radiation room itself. It felt very strange. It was probably going to be the last time I was in this room, or any radiotherapy suite for that matter.

I could go through the routine in my sleep, and often did. Address and date of birth, then getting undressed, then the couch. On this, the thirty seventh occasion, it was Gail and Clare lining me up, doing the marking, exactly as it had been on the first day. I was pleased about that, it made it strangely fitting. After the radiotherapy was complete and the accelerator was switched off, they came in and helped me down from the couch. My rucksack was now an enema-free zone, thankfully, but contained the spare trousers that had not been required on any occasion. However, it did contain a box of chocolates and a card, new additions that morning. As I thanked Gail and Clare, I handed over the card and chocolates. We had a last joke about Clare's hair and the three of us walked out of LA9.

Neal was heading in for his final session as I wandered out to the main foyer. Sitting in the semi-circular row (not *my* chair, it was occupied), I had time to take in the scene as I waited for Neal. The busy image was really no different to when I had started, eight weeks or so ago. It was just that many of the patients were different.

When Neal appeared we walked down town. It was far too early to find a pub open so we had a coffee and scone and then a browse around the bookshops. Midday eventually came but by then we were shattered. Nonetheless, we had decided some time ago to have a few drinks on this day so that was what we were going to do.

We got good seats in one of the enclosed booths in a well-known city centre pub. After the earlier scones we weren't particularly hungry so it was too early to order lunch. But we got a pint of Guinness each. After a toast to signal the end of the radiotherapy it was time to take stock. It was Neal that tried to get a handle on where we were at first. 'Jack, I assume we can take it that we are effectively cured. I know we are on the hormone therapy for a long time yet but we are expecting a positive outcome as far as I know?'

'Yes, I think so. Dr Gavasker did tell me at the start that I was high risk, with a 70-80% chance of surviving for five years. Anyhow, the internet sites tell you that this is the state of play for someone who has locally advanced prostate cancer. I don't think it is an individual assessment for me in particular.'

'No, I understand that. So we are not writing our bucket lists just yet then.'

'Definitely not. But if you were to write a bucket list, what would you have on it?'

'Not really sure. Perhaps to get through one of those self-scanners in a supermarket without having to call for help,' Neal added with a smile, thinking of the hassle of trying to buy a few groceries the night before. 'But seriously, I'm not really sure if there is anything I really feel I have to do. What about you Jack, what would you have on your bucket list?'

'Don't know, haven't thought about it, maybe I should think about it. It'll give me something to discuss with Jane over the next few weeks. Anyhow Neal, is there anything you are worried about, any loose ends from the treatment?'

'Of course there is. I'm looking forward to finishing the hormone therapy. I'm pissed off with the effect it has on my sex drive.'

'Know where you are coming from Neal,' I said, realising this was the first time we had discussed such matters. It wasn't the drink talking – we had taken less than a half pint each – but perhaps it was just the relief of reaching the end of the radiotherapy. 'I suppose it is only when we finish the hormone therapy that we will know how much damage the radiotherapy has done in that area.'

'I hadn't thought of that. Any more bad news?' Neal replied with a smile.

'There is no point worrying, we are where we are.'

'Yeah, you are right. Look at the positives. If we had been diagnosed ten or fifteen years ago we would have been in a different place. The treatment now is so much better and long term side effects from the radiotherapy are less likely than they were,' he said hopefully.

For a while we chatted about the other patients we had met, the radiotherapists and the doctors. We agreed we were lucky and could only think of positive things. Then we got talking about typical man things, sport in the main.

We struggled through two pints then decided to call it quits; we both could feel the energy draining out of us. Lunch could wait until we got home. Before heading off in our respective directions we exchanged phone numbers and email addresses and agreed we would meet every so often for a coffee. We had spent a lot of time together over the previous two months, supporting each other, discussing treatments, side effects and so on.

Going home on the train was a weird feeling. The radiotherapy was finished, yes, but the hormone therapy was to continue for a long time yet. I was pretty sure the side effects were going to be there for a while yet too.

Chapter 19

After stopping radiotherapy the next few days were bliss. Jane made sure we had very little planned and the only things planned were treats. It was only when I stopped running into Belfast every day that I realised how tired I had become. Not surprising really, hormone therapy, radiotherapy and a multitude of other drugs, not to mention the travel and the daily preparation joys.

Days became weeks and weeks became months. By late summer I was feeling a lot better. Tired often, fatigued yes, but some improvement with the radiotherapy side effects. I was led to believe that I was looking less 'drawn', a peculiar and old-fashioned term that was often used.

The first follow-up appointment in the Cancer Centre was in September. It was again with Dr Gavasker. A week or so before the appointment I had a blood sample taken for a PSA test. The score was a mighty 0.04, the lowest yet. The first thing Dr Gavasker did was to add the PSA score to my file; it didn't seem to surprise her. If the radiotherapy had done its job this was the type of score to be expected; the hope was there weren't any cancer cells left to raise the PSA level.

'Jack, how are you keeping generally? I see from your notes that you have had a tough time with side effects.'

'Yes, they have been grinding along. I think the radiotherapy ones are beginning to settle down though. I get a bit more notice when I need to go to the loo. It really is the hormone therapy side effects that are causing the problems. And they have been tough from the very start.'

We discussed the various problems, the fatigue, the very dry skin, the hot flushes and so on. Dr Gavasker reminded me that the hormone therapy is an integral part of the overall treatment but although she didn't say it explicitly, she gave me the impression that there could be some flexibility, perhaps some negotiation even. If not now, perhaps in a few months' time.

'Jack, we will put you on to a three monthly injection instead of the current monthly one you are on. I'm suggesting *Decapeptyl* SR (slow release) 11.25 mg three-monthly rather than the 3 mg you are getting each month now. While you still will have the initial surge after the injection and the fall off towards the end of the three months, there will be a longer period of stability in the mid-period. Hopefully, that might help with the severity of the side effects. But as I'm sure you know, being a testosterone-free zone is going to have its problems. We'll see how this goes and review it after three months.'

'Will I really have to be on the hormone therapy for nearly another two and a half years? It seems a very long time.'

'We will keep reviewing the position, Jack.' In reality if you come off it slightly early the increased chance of having cancer recurrence is really not very high. It's an incremental thing. Like so many things, it is a balancing act. The patient's quality of life is important and we will have to weigh up the options. Let's have this conversation again in three months and we'll see how you are getting on then. But the reality is the hormone therapy helps sort out any cancer cells floating about in the system, cells that the radiation hasn't killed. And there is no doubt that remaining on the hormones leads to improved outcomes, albeit an incremental improvement.'

On the way out of the Cancer Centre I couldn't resist the pull of the coffee dock. It still had to be decaffeinated, my gut was still too sensitive for caffeine. I managed to get my favourite seat near the door. I recognised a number of the staff coming in and out, including a couple of radiographers. I was hoping to see Gail or Clare. Perhaps it's just as well I didn't, I would recognise them instantly, but a few months after the event would they recognise me? Possibly, but I couldn't guarantee they would be able to put a name to the face. It probably is a bit like teachers meeting their former pupils. The pupils recognise the teachers immediately and then become offended when the teacher shows signs of recognition, but crucially fails to put a name to the face.

Sitting in the coffee dock, I knew I had developed a bond to this place in a strange sort of way. The eight weeks in LA9 had become a significant, if relatively short, part of my life. Finishing the dregs of my coffee, I couldn't really figure out why. There was no logical reason to it. But the one thing I was sure about was that it was the sort of thing you couldn't explain to someone who hadn't been through it. A bit like childbirth, my sister would say.

The main problem through the winter was that my skin became even drier, particularly my hands. The knuckles would bleed when it got very cold and little pieces of skin began to flake off. Bending my fingers became painful. I took to wearing gloves as much as possible. The night-time routine of thick cream within gloves couldn't be missed. But I was ticking along OK; half a stone lighter than before the radiotherapy, but people wouldn't have known what I'd been through from my appearance.

Neal was getting on well. His side effects had all but disappeared by the run up to Christmas. When we met for coffee in November he was back on caffeinated Americanos, 'mind you, Jack, just the occasional one, I don't want to push my luck. Now that I'm feeling a lot better, I'm starting to get out for a few runs. Nothing too much, three or four miles two or three times a week.'

'That's great Neal, it's a long time since I've been out for a decent walk, let alone a good run. I miss the adrenaline rush.'

I had been mulling the hormone therapy options in my head since the September appointment with Dr Gavasker. I had discussed it with Jane, but not as yet with Neal. 'Neal, I've got a review appointment coming up in the Cancer Centre around Christmas or early in the New Year. We are going to discuss the hormone therapy.'

'What is there to discuss, we are both going to be on it for another couple of years.'

'That's OK for you Neal, they don't seem to make a big difference to you but I'm finding it tough.'

'Jack, they *do* make a difference to me of course, having no testosterone is bound to, but I know what you mean. I don't get the side effects you have, or certainly not to your extent.'

'The thing is Neal, I'm hoping that I can come off the hormones early, even next summer. By then I'll have been on them for eighteen months. I'm going to bring this up at the review appointment anyway.'

The next appointment was scheduled for early January. The letter came in just before Christmas.

I put on a couple of pounds weight over Christmas but still wasn't quite back to where I was before the treatment started. Jane came along to the appointment. If it was going to involve weighing up pros and cons of stopping the hormone therapy early then she felt she really should be there. I agreed totally, she was also affected by everything that was going on. It was just over a year since diagnosis and almost a year to the day when I first discussed hormone therapy and radiotherapy with Dr Gavasker. A lot had happened in that year, but I was sure there were a few twists and turns yet to come.

After the initial hellos, Dr Gavasker offered us seats alongside her as she sat at her desk. She was facing the computer monitor, with my notes in a buff-coloured folder on the opposite side of the desk to where we were sitting. The old arrangement of the doctor being separated from the patient by a desk seemed to be a thing of the past.

'Where are we now Jack with the side effects? I know they have been a significant issue in the past.'

'They are still a significant issue. The radiotherapy side effects; the urgency to pee and the diarrhoea are really not too bad but the hormone therapy ones are still there, really unchanged in terms of their effect. The fatigue is as bad as ever, the hot flushes are probably more frequent and just look at the state of my hands.'

At that point Dr Gavasker rubbed her fingers over my hands and the knuckles in particular. 'Yes Jack, I see what you mean. They look pretty sore.'

With the bending of my fingers and the strain this caused to the dry, inflexible skin, a speck of blood oozed out from one of the many crevices that ran along the crease marks. At this point Jane chipped in, 'it is not as if we haven't tried everything to keep his skin from getting too dry, but nothing seems to work.'

Now was the time to get to the nub of the matter, 'is there any possibility of coming off the hormone therapy early?' I added, waiting anxiously for the response.

'Jack, the hormone therapy is an integral part of your overall treatment plan. I see you had your last three-monthly injection in December, so that will remain effective until well into March. By that stage you will have been on the hormones for fourteen months. We would prefer you remain on them a bit longer but at the end of the day it is your choice.'

'I think I would prefer to come off them. The last time I was here you said that if I came off them the chance of a cancer recurrence would be higher than if I was still on them, but not massively so.' Jane was nodding away, showing her support for what I was saying.

'You are correct Jack, I must warn you that there is an increased risk that cancer might reappear, but the risk is, in statistical terms, not high. Your December PSA score was 0.06 I see, so things seem to be working well. I understand your position Jack, quality of life is important too.'

We agreed in principle that I would come off the hormones, but Dr Gavasker asked me to come back and see her in two months, just before the next injection was due. 'Just for a last review of the side effects, before any important decisions are made' she said.

I felt relieved as I left the Cancer Centre. The side effects were not going to ease for at least two months, the current three-monthly hormone cycle would last that long. Winter was going to be around for a while longer and the cold contributed to the state of my hands. And there might be a hangover effect, even after the therapy was stopped. But at least I could see an end-point.

When I met Dr Gavasker in March it had become a lot milder. Not summer, but spring temperatures. But my hands were much better. So we agreed one more dose of hormone therapy which would take us up to around the eighteen month mark.

In the end I also had hormone injected in June but that was it – the final dose. It was pushing October before I started to see the side effects reduce. Dr Gavasker was happier with this arrangement. I had been on the hormone therapy for twenty months and she certainly didn't want a shorter period.

My hands improved relatively quickly and the hot flushes also became a thing of the past. The reduction of fatigue was a slower process. But things were definitely going the right direction. The weather in November was exceptionally mild so I was able to get out for the occasional walk, nothing too strenuous at first but gradually building things up. I even did a couple of miles jogging on the treadmill a few times just before Christmas. Yes things were on the move. Life was beginning to return to something approaching normal.

Chapter 20

I gradually got my energy back and memories of radiotherapy became increasing peripheral. Jane and I kept ourselves busy and, all in all, life was very much as it had been before the diagnosis. Yes, I was a couple of years older, wiser, and had some minor radiotherapy side effects reminding me from time to time what I'd been through.

Neal was in good shape too, effervescent even, much of the time. At one of our monthly coffee mornings he suggested we do the Great North Run half marathon in Tyneside the following September and raise some money for a prostate cancer charity or even for the *Friends of the Cancer Centre*. I was up for it. I enjoyed running and this would give us a target and it would also do some good, particularly if we could raise a reasonable amount of money.

We still had a good few months to build up the training and a half marathon was probably within my scope. It was certainly well within Neal's; he could do one now and a full marathon was probably within his range. He explained how to go about getting a place in the ballot. The Great North Run was so popular it was oversubscribed. We wouldn't know for sure if we would get a place for a while, but he was hopeful as he had got places before when he entered the ballot. His optimism was not misplaced, in due course our places were confirmed. The next thing to do was to consider flights and accommodation.

We planned to go over on the Saturday morning to absorb some of the atmosphere - Tyneside was the place to be on a Great North Run weekend - and return on Monday early afternoon. The run itself started on Sunday morning but it would be mid-afternoon before we were back in our base in

Newcastle. The next thing on our agenda was to book the early flight from Belfast International to Newcastle on the Saturday and book the return flight for the Monday afternoon. At this notice we were able to do it, but the Saturday outward flight was nearly full, even many months in advance. Many others with the same idea, no doubt. We booked a room each for two nights in one of the Premier Inns in the city centre, the one that overlooks the Central Motorway that we will be running down in September.

As the months passed I was feeling better and better. The running was a great boon. I think it helped me get much of my former energy back. My training runs got longer and the two of us even went on the occasional joint run. Usually along the Lagan Towpath, or if that was too busy, somewhere more isolated such as the Divis Mountain Trail.

Jane and Neal's wife, Maxine, were going to come with us to Newcastle. They also had been through a lot as we battled our way through the treatment and the accompanying side effects. The four of us met for a coffee about a month or so before the run was to take place. Neither Jane nor I had met Maxine before. She hadn't been to any of the sessions in the Cancer Centre. The pair of ladies were soon contemplating a bit of Newcastle shopping, if not on the Saturday, at least on the Monday morning. I suspected that recovery time in bed on the morning after the run would be more what Neal and I needed.

My PSA scores remained very low. Remaining low after coming off the hormone therapy is a good sign. This is when it could potentially creep up as the increasing levels of testosterone in my body could cause the proliferation of prostate cancer cells, should there be any left. All well so far, perhaps we had it beaten.

The four of us had agreed to meet for a coffee before the flight. We were all really looking forward to it.

It was an early start, but we headed for the airport in the sunshine. Each family had placed a bag in the hold. Neal and my running kits had to be considered, but space for shopping purchases on the return leg was also needed. We were both running for prostate cancer charities and also 'Friends' and had each built up a tidy sum on our *Just Giving* webpages before we left, which all added to the positive atmosphere. This made us all feel good and added to the buzz.

The flight was full, not an empty seat. Perhaps there were a number of other runners heading over. There must have been a few as the timing of this flight allowed plenty of time in Newcastle on the Saturday before the action on the Sunday. This was also the weekend when many of the 'freshers' headed over to start a new life at Newcastle's two universities. It seemed strange to have both these events, each causing a massive influx of people into the city, on the same weekend each September.

We boarded from the front steps, meaning we could see the faces of those seated near the front as we headed down the plane to our seats in rows 11 and 12. I immediately recognised the face of the girl in the seat positioned closest to the aisle in row 9. She smiled back, suggesting she at least knew my face was familiar, if not immediately able to place it in context.

It was Gail. She certainly wasn't a fresher starting the university journey. Perhaps she was on a weekend shopping expedition or she might even be doing the run itself. I could remember her making reference to being a runner during our radiotherapy chats. It was impossible to say if she was on her own or was with someone at this stage.

The flight over was short, about forty minutes max, and included a short tour over the North Sea as the plane flew over the Northumberland coastland, close to Blyth, before swinging round and landing from the east into the wind at Newcastle airport. The landing was as smooth as the rest of the flight which was a good start to our few days in the North East.

We saw Gail again on our way to baggage reclaim. Seeing Neal and I together helped jog her memory, she said she remembered us as a pair in our radiotherapy days. We had a long wait for the bags to appear so after the introductions we had time for a quick chat. Gail and her mother, Anne, were doing the Great North Run, also running for the *'Friends'* cancer charity in memory of her dad, and boyfriend Steve had come along for the weekend. Providing 'support' he chipped in, something similar to Jane and Maxine. Before leaving the airport, we all agreed we would meet up for a drink, non-alcoholic for the runners we each echoed, later that afternoon on the Quayside, somewhere not too far from the Tyne Bridge.

It was well into the morning before we got settled into the Premier Inn. They allowed us to check in early as both rooms were available. After hanging up our clothes, the four of us decided to head out for a late brunch or early lunch. We ended up in *Browns* in Grey Street. We were there so long chatting (it seemed like we were on holidays) that by the time we finished it was time to wander towards the Quayside to meet Gail and her entourage.

The Quayside area was buzzing. Junior runners were taking part in one of the satellite events that are associated with the half marathon itself. It was very crowded anywhere near the river so we wandered back up towards the city centre and ended up in a quaint real ale pub called the *Crown Posada*. In the end the four runners all had a half pint of a real ale, for each of us it was from a brewery we hadn't tried before, just to add to the experience. It was the non-combatants who had the coffee! We chatted about plans for the next day; good times to get to the start, arrangements for getting back from South Shields after the event and what we were doing on the Sunday night. Before we broke up and headed our separate ways Gail, Anne, Neal and I agreed to meet at 9.30 the next morning on the bridge that runs over the Central Motorway close to the RVI hospital. Our 'supporters' agreed to meet on the Tyne Bridge around about 11, approximately the time we would be crossing the start line. We reckoned we would reach the bridge twenty minutes or so into the run.

Jane, Maxine, Neal and myself headed out for a pasta in early evening. The pasta houses were jumping with thousands of runners carb-loading before the run. We ended up going back to our rooms reasonably early and watching television.

There was not much of a lie in the next day. Not that I got much sleep; strange bed, different sounds, worrying that I wouldn't sleep in case I was exhausted the next day. Probably no different to many of the runners.

After a light breakfast, the two of us got changed into our running gear. We were wearing our dedicated charity vests, onto which we had pinned our running numbers. My number was against a green background and Neal's had a white background. The number background colour was determined by the estimated running time we had submitted in advance to the organisers. The green assembly zones were behind the white ones. Being allocated different assembly zones was not surprising as Neal was likely to finish well before me. It took us about twenty minutes to walk to the bridge where we were meeting Gail and Anne. We got there just before them. We were all in good time. We were OK for a half hour or so, so we sat in the early morning sunshine on the Central Motorway bank overlooking the assembly zones. Gail and Anne were also wearing the distinctive yellow 'Friends' charity running tops but they had also attached a photograph of the man they were running in memory of, their dad and husband respectively. Being an experienced runner, Gail's number was on a white background but Anne was still a novice; she had a pink background and would be starting at the back – about forty thousand or so runners ahead of her when she crossed the start line. She guessed it would take her at least three hours to make it round. So what, she had worked hard and was looking forward to it.

Due to the way we were sitting, I got chatting to Gail and Neal to Anne.

'Jack, it's strange seeing you here but there are so many over for the run that I suppose I was bound to see someone I knew.'

'Yes, Neal and I saw two or three people we vaguely knew as we walked round the city yesterday.'

'Lovely city, some of my friends came over here to study. I didn't have the option, they didn't do radiotherapy here, so it had to be Ulster for me. Anyhow, it would have been hard to leave mum.'

'Nice to see her over here for the run. You didn't tell me your mum was a runner too.'

'She only started about nine months ago. It's great, it's giving her a real focus, probably for the first time since my dad died.'

Since we had arrived they had been playing music and generally giving support over the giant loudspeaker systems that had sprung up overnight along the central reservation of the motorway. The DJ announced that at 9.45, he would play *Abide with Me*, as they always did at this time each year before the run. It was widely recognised that many of the runners were running in memory of someone very close to them and this dedication was for them. *Abide with Me* started to hushed silence and it was clear that it meant a lot to many of those taking part. There were many heads bowed and I could see tears starting to trickle down Anne's cheeks.

Once the music had stopped, Gail started chatting again. 'I'm a bit worried about mum, she is way back in the pink zone. I really should run with her to make sure she gets round. It's not really fair me worrying about trying to do as well as I can and getting a fast time.'

'Nonsense Gail, it only right that you try to do well, running is your thing – you were often talking about it in LA9 and how it made you feel so good. I'll run with your mum. I am meant to be in the green zone, which is only just ahead of your mum's pink zone. I'll drop back into the pink zone and keep your mum company.'

'Would you Jack, it would be great if you could. But I know it would be asking a lot.'

'No problem at all. I'll enjoy the company. Anyhow, if you are looking for a bit of competitive company, you and Neal can start out together.'

After a bit more chat, Neal and Gail headed into the white zone, well ahead of where Anne and I entered the pink zone. Once we were installed in our assembly zones the adrenaline started to get going and the DJ got us into warm-up mode. Around 11am Anne and I crossed the start line, probably about fifteen minutes after the other two. Two miles into the run Anne and I were still together, high-fiving Steve, Jane and Maxine on the Tyne Bridge.

The priority for Anne and I was to finish. We had different targets; Anne was doing it for her husband Brian and I was doing it for myself, proving that I could get back to normal after having cancer. We were still together as we entered South Shields and reached the sea, just one mile to go up the hill and into the wind, the *Red Arrows* doing their display to our right over the North Sea. We crossed the finish line together, two hours and forty five minutes after crossing the start line. By the time we got our breath back Anne was in tears. The occasion and the fulfilment of all those hours training had got to her now that she had made it. Gail and Neal were there waiting. Gail hugged her mother and they both started crying. Tears of joy. They had done it. Neal and Gail had also crossed the line together. The big difference being it took them less than two hours. They are experienced runners so this was hardly a surprise.

After a long wait, we got back to Newcastle on the Metro. Before splitting in Northumberland Street we arranged to go for a quick celebratory drink before we got showered and tidied up. While Neal and I were staying overnight, Anne and Gail were getting the late flight back to Derry. They both had work in the morning. Even worse, Gail had the long drive back up to the Cancer Centre to contend with as well. Still, I had the feeling she would be going home content. Yes, she had achieved a lot over the weekend, but I think she would be of the impression her mum had achieved even more. Her dad wouldn't be forgotten, but I was fairly sure she would be content in the knowledge that her mum was ready to move on.

No sooner had Anne and Gail departed, Maxine and Jane appeared. They had spent the afternoon in Eldon Square, shopping and generally chilling out. They had had a ball. Neither was interested in running and neither really understood what it was all about. They had done their bit by seeing us over the Tyne Bridge a few hours earlier, but that was as far as it went.

By the time we were changed and heading out that evening I was starting to stiffen up quite a bit. The buzz and sense of achievement more than made up for it. After a few beers the pain and stiffness were a long way away.

On the plane the next afternoon I thought things couldn't really be much better. We had had a great weekend and achieved much more than I could have thought was possible many months earlier when the radiotherapy, and its side effects, was at its height. The hormone therapy side effects were also distant memories. Seeing Gail, a stalwart of LA9, seemed to signal my own particular closure to those tumultuous days. Yes, things were good, the rest of my life started now.

Epilogue

Looking back I realised that I had drifted through the cancer treatment in a bit of a daze. It now seems almost unreal. It's possible that is how many of us cope with it. I seem to have come out the other end in not too bad a state. A number of people have said that the diagnosis and treatment didn't seem to bring out the fear factor in me, or even the anger, that a cancer diagnosis often does. Maybe I've been through too much or perhaps it's a personality thing.

Yes, some of the side effects are still there, intermittent or otherwise. And new ones come along at intervals. Perhaps my very low white blood cell count is in this category. Hard to say whether it's down to a side effect of some of the medication or whether it is because some of the bone marrow that makes the blood cells has been zapped by the radiotherapy.

Maybe it is actually tougher being the partner, the supporter of the patient. Always trying to be positive, encouraging, but worrying underneath it all. And of course, expected to be a pillar of support, irrespective of how they feel on the inside. And not always seeing at first hand the wealth of support patients benefit from and the positive nature of so much of the treatment. The Cancer Centre deserves its five stars for that.

Neal, Gail and I hope to do the next Belfast Marathon for the 'Friends' charity. Not the full distance – certainly too much for me, if not for the others – but as part of a relay.

Neal and I still get our PSA checked, but not as frequently as before. The readings are still negligible so all seems to be going well. We have been lucky in having a type of cancer that could be treated at a local centre of excellence and also at a time when there has been rapid and significant progress in developing new and better treatments. Equally importantly in the case of prostate cancer, new treatments with much reduced side effects.

Cancer is still a hateful disease, even the word is enough to frighten so many people. And not everyone is lucky and able to benefit from an early diagnosis and state of the art treatment. These are the targets but we are not there yet - if it had been pancreatic as opposed to prostate cancer things would probably have been very different.

Mandy died about a year after her treatment was finished. She was unlucky and she had one of those types of cancer that often presents too late. Sean is not doing that well either, perhaps he was just too late in seeking help.

Gail is still working away, doing her bit to brighten up the day for those in her expert care. She is now engaged to Steve and things are going very well, good for her. Anne is doing well too.

My next check-up in the Cancer Centre is almost due. Jane will be coming with me. For some strange reason I still feel a real positive buzz when I enter those revolving doors. It is only by being through it all that you can really understand how important a resource it is. What a place.

Friends of the Cancer Centre

Friends of the Cancer Centre, based at the heart of the Cancer Centre at Belfast City Hospital, is a leading local cancer charity working to support cancer patients and their families across Northern Ireland. Friends of the Cancer Centre funds life-saving and life-changing projects throughout the Cancer Centre which make a real and meaningful difference to the lives of thousands of people across Northern Ireland.

The work of Friends of the Cancer Centre focuses on three key areas – patient comfort and care, clinical care, and research – and last year alone the charity put nearly £1.5 million back into the Cancer Centre. The charity relies entirely on donations and on the generosity of people in Northern Ireland who raise funds to support its work.